THE STORY TELLER

BEGINNINGS

May 12, 2001

Pastor Jen,

Congratulations on your Graduation! We are so proud to know you and be part of your congregation. You have truly been touched by God to lead us!

Thank you!
Love,
Seth, Lisa and Katie Mapes

THE STORY TELLER

BEGINNINGS

A Gallery of Biblical Portraits

Steve Stephens

PROMISE
PRESS
An Imprint of Barbour Publishing

© 1998 by Steve Stephens

ISBN 1-57748-678-1

Cover illustration: Lookout Design Group
www.lookoutdesign.com

Published by Promise Press, an imprint of Barbour Publishing, Inc., P.O. Box 719, Uhrichsville, Ohio 44683, http://www.barbourbooks.com

ecpa Member of the
Evangelical Christian
Publishers Association

Printed in the United States of America.

DEDICATION

To my three wonderful children:
Brittany, Dylan, and Dusty,
who have filled my life
with love, laughter, and challenge.
May you walk long with Garden-Maker
and listen closely to Promise-Keeper.
I love you!

ACKNOWLEDGMENTS

The author gratefully acknowledges those whose lives and support have been integral to this retelling of the stories of Garden-Maker and Promise-Keeper.

- My beloved wife Tami for listening, loving, giving, encouraging, and everything else.

- Sue Powers and Linda Graham for patiently typing and retyping.

- The Monday Night Growth Group (Dan and Sue, Jim and Allison, Dan and Shanni, Todd and Monica) for discussing the early drafts.

- Mike DeBoer, Jim Allison, and Chip MacGregor for reading and commenting.

- David Sanford for encouraging and agenting.

- Paul Ingram for patiently editing

- Loren Fischer for his theological input and shepherding.

- Stan Ellison for teaching and outlining the Old Testament with simplicity and clarity.

- Grandma Blanche for praying for me daily.

INTRODUCTION

Genesis is the beginning.

Genesis is also about beginnings. It is the book of the beginnings of life and truth and evil and hope. It is one of the most significant portions of the most consequential book the world has ever known.

However, in an age of computers and television, the ancient stories are always in danger of being overfamiliar or neglected or boxed in a smugly ordered view of reality. Some say the stories are obscure or antiquated or even irrelevant. I believe they hold powerful messages that percolate from a wellspring of eternal truth.

So I have put on storyteller's garb, not to translate or paraphrase the Scriptures of Judaism and Christianity; certainly not to rewrite or improve upon the accounts. I would simply distill thirty of these stories in a setting I hope is vivid and interesting.

I came to this project through prayer, study, and much soul searching. Translations were read, commentaries considered, words cross-referenced, encyclopedias examined, atlases plotted, histories compared, and interpretations debated. I have tried to remain faithful enough to history and geography that the reader will not lose sight of the facts behind the words. Yet the larger concern is to show that Father and Mother, Merchant and Walker and Shepherdess—even First-Born—are essentially like us. As the old storyteller by the fire might say, these are our stories. I hope our stories are inspiring to those who have never heard them and to those who know the biblical details by heart. Mostly I hope many will dust off their Bibles and discover the originals. Those who open their hearts to the truths in Genesis may ultimately find themselves drawing closer to him who is Garden-Maker and Promise-Keeper.

Beginnings is the first in a series of four story-prose interpretations of the narratives of what Christians call the Old Testament. If you enjoy these stories I hope you will look for *Leaders, Kingdoms,* and *Promises.*

PART 1
THE GARDEN-MAKER

TABLE OF CONTENTS
THE GARDEN-MAKER

PROLOGUE

It was late.

Most of the people were asleep, exhausted from a long day of labor under the scorching sun. But just as days were unfailingly hot, nights turned crisp, almost frosty. A small circle of adults and their children clung to the crackling fire outside their tents, the women comparing problems of the home, the men talking about the new lambs.

The attitude around the fire was relaxed, friendly, hushed. . .and expectant.

An old man with a long, gray beard stepped into the firelight's gentle radiance. He slowly circled the flames, silently, seriously pacing his sandaled steps. His plain wool robe brightened in the glow of the firelight. He was thin, in the way of old men who have grown lean and hardened by active life. A hundred finely etched wrinkles spun across his weathered face from a coarse and indifferently combed tangle of white beard, but his eyes were young and clear.

The old man stopped absentmindedly and turned away, as if to contemplate the dim shadows cast by the flames. A few children had dozed in the cozy warmth. So had a few adults, though they would not have admitted it. Now they rubbed the sleep from their eyes and waited. Their conversations died down.

They waited quietly, patiently for the words that had been promised.

But the words seemed not quite ready; the stories he had to tell were not to be recited lightly. He stopped and breathed deeply.

Older hearers knew these stories as their own, and they longed to hear them once more, and longed for their children to remember them from the lips of the elder. They sat cross-legged on the dry, sandy ground. It had been over an hour now, yet no one complained.

The storyteller had spent years studying and memorizing every sentence. He was said to have actually seen and read the sacred scrolls that now lay sealed in the caves northwest of the salty sea. Those ancient scrolls. . . each letter perfectly inscribed. . .not an article or preposition or conjunction out of place.

All the listeners, young and old, thrilled at the exploits of their forefathers. These words were history and more, for they gave the people purpose and perspective. The storyteller's pure, simple images of the past enlightened the present and forged hope for the future. Only the foolish disregarded them.

The storyteller looked to the black star-splashed sky and closed his eyes. Figures about the fire leaned forward, for they knew the time was near. The fire burst red and yellow sparks into the dark air. From the distant rocky hills came the unearthly wail of a jackal, in its hunt for food by the light of a sliver of moon.

The old man opened his eyes.

He began to speak.

BEGINNINGS ARE CURIOUS,
BECAUSE IN LIFE IT'S DIFFICULT
TO KNOW WHEN A STORY
ACTUALLY STARTS.

CHAPTER 1

THE GARDEN

There was a time before time began when the blue planet was black, pitch-black without a hint of light anywhere. It hung still and silent in an empty universe of ultimate darkness.

Suddenly quiet was shattered as time's wheels jerked into motion.

Suddenly the blackness was vanquished, and light flashed through space.

The light cut waters from the sky to bathe an infant world. Like a baby awakened from sleep and now hungry, this little one exploded with energy and desire.

Mountains burst from the sea.

Rivers rushed down their sides.

Tender green shoots sprouted into immense virgin forests.

Lands were carpeted with the greens and blues and reds and pinks and yellows of growing things varied beyond imagining. Birds criss-crossed the blue sky in a simple ballet of feather and song. In that first night, a celebration of suns and stars exploded across the ebony shroud.

The blue planet was alive!

Everything was perfect, but nothing else could quite compare with the garden. Somewhere on a bed of softest moss, between the mighty trees and the gurgling stream, lay the form. In all that scene of life, only the form did not seem to live. It was not dead, but its eyes did not open. It had a mouth that did not speak, and there was no breath. A curious rabbit poked the form with its pink nose. A lioness licked at the face as if this were a new cub. Even the horse wondered, though of more interest to the horse was a patch of tender grass by the water.

This form was special. So why would it not awaken? Let it rise up and play.

To the form the world remained black and silent. There was no feeling, no smell, no taste.

Unusual gray-white clouds gathered and cast a shadow upon the lifeless form. The air cooled slightly and the world paused. The animals backed slowly away, not afraid but watchful and reverent. Even the horse became alert, with only an occasionally nip at the shoots around his hooves. A jagged light from the clouds split the sky. With exquisite aim it pierced and exploded inside the form.

Then the lightning was gone, the clouds faded into their blue background, and Man moved his right hand. A gentle breeze brushed his lips and they parted just a crack. The animals moved closer. The man's nose twitched and his jaw dropped as he involuntarily gasped for air.

Life.

Sweet air filled the mouth and lungs of Man. Slowly the eyes began to see. Then they quickly shut for there was too much to see! Colors and textures overwhelmed him. He blinked and squinted at the intensity of the brightness of his surroundings.

Man rubbed his face and stretched, extending his arms fully above his head to work his new muscles. The brightness still hurt, and he squeezed his eyes shut against the dizzying kaleidoscope.

A little more time with darkness was needed. His consciousness drifted away in secure peace.

Eventually a birdsong filled his ears and a scratchy tongue tickled his face. He shook his head and looked into the face of the large, furry animal who thought this cub needed mothering. The immense face insistently nuzzled his neck.

It was a beautiful day.

The sky was the clearest and palest of blues, the landscape a vivid palette of greens. Man stood up and scanned his surroundings. An apple tree, heavy with shiny yellow fruit, stood beside a massive oak, stately and thick with moss. Wild roses and pure white lilies grew on the bank of a quiet pond. He dipped his fingers into the clear water and watched the circular ripples scatter from his touch. Shafts of sunlight hit the surface at just the right angle to turn the liquid silver.

Now Man was drawn to look into the water. He stared at the strong, tall figure reflected there. His sparkling brown eyes were pure and hid none of his thoughts. His face was calm and relaxed.

No worry lines marked his brow.

No tension knotted his jaw.

No fear tightened his lips.

That day Man wandered all of the garden. Everything amazed him so—the brilliant purple of the crocus, the cry of the high circling hawk, the pungent smell of the aloe plant, the mouth-puckering sourness of the lemon and the softness of the newborn lamb's wool.

When his senses could be fed no more, he reclined on a grassy tuft, leaned against a young palm, and breathed deeply of the fresh, clean air. The sun kissed the horizon, splashing out an incredible splay of colors. As the garden slipped into darkness new and mysterious sounds engulfed Man.

Crickets chirped; frogs croaked; owls hooted.

Man knew none of these noises, and he searched for their sources, but each was too carefully cloaked by the night. In the black sky a delicate crescent of brightness ruled over thousands of glittering stars. He was transfixed by the magnitude of it all as he drifted into tranquil, contented sleep.

Days and nights passed. Each day was a beautiful encore of the first, and each night Man dreamed a world as wonderful as his waking paradise. Each dawn he awoke well-rested and eager to embrace new adventures.

He knew no disappointments.

No frustration.

No heartbreak.

One day as Man strolled barefoot through the shade of mighty willows and cedars and oaks, he considered how they towered to the heavens. He grabbed hold of a low branch and swung effortlessly onto a massive branch. Things looked different from above, he noticed. So he climbed higher. After scrambling fearlessly from foothold to foothold he reached a spot where he could poke his head out into the sunshine. What a joy it was to look over all that Garden-Maker had planted and given him. It was a vast place, but he could identify in the distance the four great rivers that marked the outer boundaries. And he could squint his eyes, strain forward and glimpse other lands between the rivers and the horizon. He had walked along the rivers, but had never really paid attention to what lay outside.

Now he studied these distance places—and shivered.

They looked so lonely, so empty of the presence of Garden-Maker.

It was an unpleasant sensation, a foreboding premonition of great darkness.

His head swirled as he rapidly descended the tree. He could neither catch his breath or slow his heart until his feet again trod the fertile forest floor. Here he belonged, surrounded by love and purpose.

His path took him into the brightness of a wildflower-strewn meadow. He lie on his back among the varicolored blooms and watched the clouds float lazily across the azure sky. The warm sun touched his bare chest as he closed his eyes to enjoy a light breeze perfumed with lilac and honeysuckle.

He ate his fill from a vast offering of the most delicious and satisfying fruit, all of which seemed to be in a constant state of ripe perfection. A bubbling stream cascaded through the garden, collecting here and there in crystal pools of refreshing water that quenched Man's deepest thirst. Animals of every type lived by the stream—gazelles, tigers, a mother bear and her two cubs, a few rabbits, a lone coyote. All rested peacefully in the lush grasses of the gently sloping bank.

It was along this stream where Man would come each morning to meet Garden-Maker. As the sun peaked over the eastern horizon and the birds began their daybreak song, the two walked along the gentle stream and talked of many things. They laughed and shared their hearts without fear or mistrust or secrets. Mostly Man listened closely, for Garden-Maker had many things to teach. When Man had a question, Garden-Maker answered.

Man was perfectly content.

Garden-Maker smiled.

A HEART ACHES
WHEN IT HAS NO ONE TO LOVE,
FOR IT IS IN GIVING
THAT A HEART LEARNS JOY.

CHAPTER 2

THE WOMAN

It's hard to say when it actually started.

It began slowly and quietly—an ache in the chest, a tug on the heart, an emptiness of soul.

It felt as if something was missing.

But how can that be? The man had everything he ever wanted, and if he wished for more, all he had to do was ask Garden-Maker.

But. . .still. . .something was missing.

Along the stream where the cattails grew high and the willows hung low, the man sat silently on the bank and watched the animals drink. Nearby a majestic lion rested in the ferns and daylilies. A lioness playfully purred and nuzzled her wet nose into the dark mane of her muscular mate. The man walked away, head bent, wondering why he had no companion of his own kind.

The man grew introspective and sullen. Small droplets collected in the corners of his eyes, making the world blurry and his loneliness more intense. The only thing that still brought a smile to his face was the early morning walks with Garden-Maker.

One day, as the sun first filtered through the forest and animals drowsily opened their eyes, the man spoke his mind.

"Garden-Maker?"

"Yes? I am here."

"Something deep inside hurts, and I can't get it to stop," the man sighed. "I feel so alone. The giraffe has a partner. The ox has a partner. Even the tiny mouse has a partner. Every animal has a partner—except me."

"But you have me. We walk and talk each morning. Anytime you call, I come. Anything you want, I supply."

"But you are Garden-Maker. You live beyond the sky and hold the stars in your hands. You're infinite and eternal and all-powerful. I need you, but I also need someone I can touch—someone like me."

"I know," Garden-Maker said with a smile. "Now you understand that I have not finished your making. Lie down and I will complete my creation."

The man knew something miraculous was about to happen as a heavy sleep pulled him into dreamless oblivion. Garden-Maker looked at the man asleep on the grass and felt tender compassion.

Deep into the man's side reached Garden-Maker. With skilled hands he painlessly removed small slivers of Man's heart and soul. These he shaped into something like Man, and yet unlike. A smaller form was molded, less muscular. The skin was softer, and the features more delicate. Yet that body also was designed with strengths Man's body did not have, and the soul was a special mixing of nurturing love and rocklike resolve. Man had weaknesses; Garden-Maker had not intended that he, of all the creatures, should stand in isolation.

Now would come a completer.

Dark hair flowed around her shoulders in gentle waves and half-curls. The Garden-Maker formed elegant lines and shapely curves, gracefully integrating them into pleasing symmetry. When Garden-Maker finished, he stood back from his creation and smiled.

"Good. Very good."

All was ready except for the last and most important detail. Without it the creation of this new being would be meaningless. Garden-Maker bent over the lifeless form, breathed into her mouth and energized her new lungs with his spirit.

A heart pounded. A soul stirred.

A shudder in the chest spread to hands and feet.

Woman was alive.

When the man opened his eyes, he rubbed his side. It felt strange. He looked and saw a white scar marking his tanned body. He ran his hand over the raised line running down his right side, wondering.

Then all questions faded. Less than an arm's reach away, an angelic creature lay asleep in the grass. Clear, deep, dark eyes opened and this new being gazed honestly, calmly into his heart.

The man reached out tentatively. He touched the lips. He ran his fingers through the long hair. Never had he seen quite so lovely a creature, even in this place. They stood and without a word walked together through the garden.

"Look," he said, pointing to a doe and buck drinking peacefully at the stream.

"What are they?" asked his companion as they approached the animals.

"I call them deer," said Man, and reached out to stroke the neck of the doe. "Aren't they beautiful?"

"It's all beautiful," she said, "and what are those?" Bits of yellows and orange and azure fluttered in the breeze.

"Butterflies."

"And those?"

"Horses."

"And those. . .and those. . .and those. . ." She dashed about, pointing to every animal in sight. Man laughed at her delight and curiosity. One by one he shared the names of all the creatures she saw.

"So what am I?" the companion turned to ask. Man glanced down at the scar on his side.

"You are part of me and I am part of you."

"Do I have a name?"

"You are woman."

"Woman. I like my name. It is like your name, yet different."

"We are companions and shall always walk together."

"Always," she promised. "Now, what are those?" she asked, pointing to a splash of red at the edge of the stream.

"They are berries," he laughed, "sweet and delicate and wonderful to eat." Woman took his hand.

"Show me," she said.

Man was sure the berries had never tasted better than they did this day.

He gave her gifts of fruit and flowers. She accepted them with a carefree laugh and an affectionate gaze at her mate. He seemed so kind and gentle and generous. She reached out and slipped her hand into his once more. They interweaved their fingers, and he smiled a joyful, innocent, embracing smile.

They climbed high in the mighty oaks to see the baby birds asleep in their lofty perches.

They danced amid hyacinths in the bright meadow.

They smelled the thornless roses.

They stood under the waterfall and felt the waters cascade off their faces and shoulders and backs.

They ate and drank and laughed and played.

Then they sat side by side and watched the sun slip below the horizon. As the light faded, he placed his arm around her shoulders and pulled her close. The ache in his chest was gone, the tug on his heart had lost its pull, and the emptiness of his soul had been filled to overflowing.

The man ran the fingers of his free hand over the thin raised scar and mouthed a silent "Thank you" to Garden-Maker. Together, Man and Woman watched a silver circle of a moon peek through the branches of an apple tree. Then they slept in each other's arms as stars sang the song of the Garden-Maker.

PRIDE AND THE PUSH FOR POWER
ULTIMATELY PIERCE
THE FABRIC OF THE UNIVERSE,
RIPPING PERFECTION'S GOLDEN CLOTH AND
FORMING THE RAGGED EDGE OF ANARCHY.

CHAPTER 3

THE REVOLT

Far away, beyond the sky and beyond time, dwelt Garden-Maker. His mighty hand and kind heart ruled every corner of the universe. Threads of peace were woven into the fabric of his makings—

What has breath and what has no breath.

What moves and what is still.

What can be seen and what is beyond the keenest vision.

Surrounding Garden-Maker were thousands upon thousands of angels. And the greatest of all was known as Shining-One—for his brilliance outshone the stars. He was iridescently beautiful and immensely powerful and wonderfully intelligent, more so than Man or Woman could ever hope to be.

Other angels were drawn to Shining-One by his winsome, hypnotic eloquence. They began to think of him as their leader, rather than the Garden-Maker himself. Shining-One did not dissuade them, for he had grown restless. His once-pure heart was tainted by self-love. His loyalty to Garden-Maker wavered.

Shining-One thought he could keep his heart hidden from Garden-Maker. He quietly wandered the universe sparking disorder and spreading discontent. He mumbled and complained and criticized and questioned. He had not fooled Garden-Maker. Most of the angels were shocked to see Shining-One's heart turn dark, but many were still taken in by his smooth rhetoric and baseless promises. He whispered lies and boasted. He gathered his confused followers and led them into an ultimate deception. Perhaps he had come to believe it himself, and that was his fatal mistake.

"I will live on the throne beyond the sky," said Shining-One. "I will hold the stars in my hands." His voice was loud and confident. "I will be infinite and eternal and all-powerful. I will be the new Garden-Maker," he shouted into the blackness of space. "Come with me," he whispered among his followers. "You need not be slaves to Garden-Maker's plan. I will give you freedom, and you too will be great."

The dark-hearted angels cheered, and Shining-One gloated. Together they planned and schemed, looking for the perfect place and time to overthrow Garden-Maker. Weapons were stockpiled and strategies plotted. Good now had its enemy and innocence its thief. The universe divided and every virtue had its counterpoint.

At a prearranged moment the battle cry echoed from planet to planet. Shining-One led the revolt. Dark angels charged Garden-Maker, and loyal angels held their ground. Flaming swords crashed against each other, scattering searing sparks across newborn galaxies.

Suddenly blinding light shook the stars from their foundations. Garden-Maker raised his arms and time stopped.

"Enough!"

The flaming swords of the rebels scorched the hands that grasped them, leaving them screeching in agony. Then the weapons simply disappeared. Those who would replace Garden-Maker learned that it is hopeless to challenge the one who is above all. In the spiritual realms there was sudden, absolute silence. Garden-Maker's eyes met the eyes of his opponents. Each quickly looked away, even Shining-One.

"Be gone!"

Garden-Maker's deep voice quaked through the core of every living and nonliving entity of his infinitely expanding creation. The followers of Shining-One realized that their combined strength could not extinguish a single ray of Garden-Maker's infinite power. Their greed and foolishness had damned them. In hysterical panic, the dark angels broke rank and fled to the deepest, most unexplored edges of the universe. Yet, in supreme arrogance or desperation, Shining-One set his face and refused to budge.

"Oh, Shining-One," Garden-Maker called, "why have you established yourself as my adversary?"

"I wanted to prove that I can also rule the universe."

"But that is not your role."

"I refuse my role!" The words of Shining-One were spit out in defiant hatred.

"You have chosen a different path, so be gone from my presence."

"But your presence is everywhere."

"Choose a place, then and it will be yours until the end of this age."

"I choose that young planet," said Shining-One with a half grin. He knew the affection with which the Garden-Maker regarded this odd little ball. Now he could bargain, for Garden-Maker would never give up this world.

"I demand the third world from the small sun. The blue planet. The Garden and Man and Woman."

If Garden-Maker was surprised it did not show. Shining-One was unprepared for the answer:

"It is yours, but you may not harm the two I have created."

"May I speak to them?"

"So you wish to lie to them and deceive them?"

"I wish to give them alternatives."

"You may test them, but not in your shining form. You no longer deserve your beauty so I will give you a more fitting form. You are a dragon, a serpent, a lowly snake; those are the shapes you must now take."

The Shining-One turned his back on Garden-Maker and started to walk away. Then he turned.

"I have lost this battle, but there will come another battle."

"Yes," said Garden-Maker. "There will come another battle."

Lightning flashed and thunder rolled. Time began to move again, and a thousand suns exploded. The heart of Shining-One melted, and he ran in terror from the realms of Garden-Maker's home.

Far away a snake slithered through the garden grass and sunned itself on an open spot near the shadow of a large tree.

LIFE IS FILLED WITH CHOICES;
GOOD CHOICES GO UNNOTICED,
WHILE BAD CHOICES TWIST
THE COURSE OF HISTORY.

CHAPTER 4

THE CHOICE

In a small clearing, not far from a stream, grew the most beautiful tree Woman had seen in the garden. Smooth silver bark covered its thick trunk, and songbirds nested in its large, spreading branches. Golden leaves sparkled in the afternoon sun as she sat on the grass, pondering the tree.

"It's lovely, isn't it?"

She almost didn't hear the voice, so engrossed was she in the remarkable tree before her. Now she glanced at the large serpent that spoke. Man had not introduced her to this.

"It's perfect," she answered in an awed whisper.

"Especially the fruit," the snake added.

The woman nodded as she contemplated the bright red globes of fruit hanging from the limbs. There must have been nearly a hundred of them, each about the size of her hand.

"I've always wondered. . . ," he began.

"Wondered?"

"I've wondered why Garden-Maker deprives you of this most delectable creation."

Woman's eyes didn't move from the fruit.

"Is it good?"

"Sublime," Shining-One hissed as he casually slithered toward his hole at the foot of the tree.

She sat a little longer, staring at the fruit, questions filling her mind. Then she got up and rejoined Man, who wrestled playfully with a lion in a nearby meadow.

"What does the fruit feel like?" she asked.

"What fruit?"

"The fruit from the golden tree."

"I don't know, but don't touch it."

"Don't you ever wonder whether it's hard like a nut or soft like a peach?"

"No," the man said, slowly shaking his head. "The Garden-Maker said if we eat it we will die. My heart grew dark at his words. I know it is better not to approach it."

"Then why did Garden-Maker plant it. . .and in the very center of the garden?"

"I only know the rule: 'Do not eat!' "

"Aren't you a little curious?"

"Garden-Maker gave us a single rule; we can do whatever else we please."

"It pleases Garden-Maker if we do not even think about it."

But the woman could not forget the fruit. The next day she found herself again sitting on the grass, staring at the golden tree.

"Are you sure. . . ?" began Shining-One. "Did Garden-Maker really say you couldn't eat from this tree?"

"He said if we ate the fruit, or even got too close, we'd die."

"That's ridiculous. How could a piece of fruit kill anyone? I've tasted it. It didn't hurt me."

"But you're different."

"Not as different as you think," Shining-One chuckled. "Come closer and give it a little touch. What could be wrong with just a touch?"

The woman inched forward, slowly raising her index finger toward the bright red fruit until there was contact. She flinched but nothing happened. The day remained bright.

"You see," hissed Shining-One. "You can't always believe what Garden-Maker says. He has his secrets. There's a lot he doesn't tell."

"He tells us everything we need to know," the woman said with renewed confidence.

"Did he say that with this fruit you would know his secrets, secrets of the universe? Why does he withhold his wisdom?"

"All the secrets of the universe?"

"With just one small bite."

"I need to ask Man about this."

"Do you need his permission? Can't you decide for yourself? Wouldn't you like to know more than he?"

"I can make my own choices," the woman insisted with a touch of anger. "But he's my companion. We make our choices together."

"But this is just a taste."

"The Garden-Maker said a taste will kill."

"If a touch doesn't kill, why would a taste?"

Shining-One slipped away from the tree. Then he turned and added: "Think about it."

The woman's eyes returned to the fruit. She tried counting, just in curiosity, how many of the beautiful globes hung from the tree. Impulsively, she reached up and touched the nearest fruit. Again, nothing happened. She cautiously wrapped her fingers around it and squeezed gently. The fruit was cool and firm.

She pulled, but the stem clung stubbornly to the branch.

Then she tugged with all her strength, and the fruit broke free with a snap. She fell back onto the grass with it tight in her hand. She sat up and looked at the bright red fruit. Picking a golden leaf from the tree, she shined the fruit until it glowed.

Carefully she drove her fingernails through the firm skin. It broke into halves. Dark red juice spilled down her arms as she placed her nose near and smelled its sweet aroma. Her mouth watered as she brought the fruit right up to her lips. Then she stopped.

"No, I can't do this," she said to herself. "I should just throw it away and get out of here. Or maybe I should take these two halves to Garden-Maker; I'll explain and apologize and ask his forgiveness."

She paused and a look of sadness crossed her face.

"But it's too late. I've already touched it, so I might as well just eat it."

She closed her eyes and bit through the ripe red skin into the tender fruit. She smiled and juice trickled from the corners of her mouth and down her delicate chin. It tasted wonderfully sweet and soothing and satisfying. It melted on her tongue like honey and slid easily down her throat.

Then the woman's face twisted, her lips puckered, and she gagged. Her throat burned and her chest rumbled violently. She threw down the uneaten fruit and spit out what was left in her mouth.

Her head spun.

New and confusing thoughts raced through her mind.

Where was peace? Where was innocence?

Wicked choices flashed before her—choices she suddenly knew would hurt Garden-Maker, hurt the garden, hurt the animals, hurt Man, and hurt even herself. And for some reason she wanted to do all those things. The ability to cause pain presented itself in a hundred different forms, forms she never knew existed:

Lying. Cheating. Hating.

Fighting. Stealing. Killing.

Her desires were choking out the flowers all around. Why were her thoughts so dark? Why did the garden seem suddenly so distorted? She looked at her body and saw with shock that she was exposed for anyone to see. She grabbed up some large leaves, worked some strong fibers from the stems of a nearby plant and wrapped them around her waist. Fear made her tremble.

She felt ugly and evil and alone.

"Where is Man?" she cried. "He must hold me and protect me and tell me everything will be all right."

So she ran frantically through the garden—calling, yelling, crying, until her heart pounded out a terrified beat, her sides ached, and her body dripped.

Man watched her approach with concern, for he was enjoying a view of the beautiful garden from high in the upper branches of a stately oak. He had been looking again past the four rivers, thankful that he need not exist in that barren world. Suddenly a strange wail of pain and panic tore through his peaceful afternoon. It was unlike anything he'd ever heard before. He looked down and saw Woman racing wildly through the forest.

Something was wrong, terribly wrong. The man climbed down the tree quickly and enclosed Woman in his arms. She collapsed there, her body shaking and her breathing ragged. Tears streamed down her face.

"Shining-One. He tricked me. I'm so sorry. It tasted good, but it's so wrong. . . . I'm so sorry. I'm lost. . .I'm dying! Forgive me!"

The man looked at her in confusion and disbelief. It was Woman, but not the same as before. Her face was contorted, her forehead furrowed, her eyes haunted, her jaw clenched. He did not understand all she said, but he knew she was irretrievably changed. She had broken the command. What she had lost could not be regained.

The man pulled away and was silent. Tears formed in his eyes and rolled freely down his ruddy cheeks. He sat on the grass and looked away from the woman as heavy sobs shook his chest. His love was lost to him.

Unless. . .

Man took a deep breath and turned toward Woman. He reached out, gently brushing tangled hair from her frightened face. Taking her trembling hands, he pulled her close and softly kissed her moist lips.

The sun had started to set when she fell into exhausted sleep. He let loose of her hands and silently walked the path toward the center of the garden.

"What should I do?" Man asked himself. Normally he would have waited and addressed this question to Garden-Maker in the morning. But this was something Garden-Maker could not know, not yet. Now he must follow his own counsel.

"The woman broke the rule of the golden tree. Garden-Maker will kill her, or cast her into the barren lands beyond the rivers. She could not survive there alone. I can't let him do that! She's my companion."

Why did it suddenly seem Garden-Maker was so unfair, even cruel?

"I told her that eating the fruit was wrong. But now she has eaten. Should I abandon the woman to her fate or share this too with her, protecting her from Garden-Maker?"

Choices.

Difficult choices.

Choices with horrible consequences.

Oh, it hurt the head to think of them all. Now he must act quickly and decisively and alone.

He stood before the golden tree, looking at it closely for the first time. Then he deliberately reached and violently plucked a fruit from a golden limb. He stared at it in the palm of his hand, thinking of Garden-Maker, thinking of Woman.

With intense pain he cried out.

"Why?"

He raised the fruit above his head and squeezed it until it split open. The sweet juice ran down his hand and dripped into his open mouth. Shining-One watched and smiled.

GRASPING OUR DESIRES
FREQUENTLY INVOLVES
LOSING OUR DREAMS.

CHAPTER 5

THE EXILE

Horrible, monstrous nightmares haunted their sleep. Man and Woman tossed and turned on the grass beneath the golden tree as the moon rose high on a star-studded canopy. Their stomachs ached and their throats burned as fever drenched their bodies in hot, sticky sweat.

Through the long night the couple dreamed they ran madly across windswept plains, pursued by a hideous creature. They ran and hid and ran, so that they awoke with tired legs and broken spirits.

Then they ran and hid once more.

As dawn's first rays shown above the eastern mountains, Garden-Maker walked the bank of the stream to the meeting place. On a large granite boulder he waited. He scanned the meadow and called their names with a voice that reached every crevice of the garden.

He expected no answer. He saw where they watched, but still he waited and called.

Finally, across the meadow the bushes stirred. Garden-Maker walked calmly toward the rustling leaves.

"Why are you hiding?"

The man stood, but kept the foliage between them.

"I'm sorry," he said. "We heard footsteps and were afraid of your anger."

"I love you. Why would I be angry?"

Man averted his eyes and said nothing.

"You both look so tired," said Garden-Maker.

"We did not sleep well," said Woman, though she did not come into view.

"Were there bad dreams?"

34

"How did you know?" asked Man.

"I know all things."

"Then you know. . . ?"

"You thought I would not? How little you know me yet."

"You know we broke the rule of the golden tree?"

"Yes," Garden-Maker said sadly. "Tell me why."

"I did it for Woman. She ate the fruit. I couldn't bear her death."

"She broke the rule of the golden tree, and there are consequences."

"But the consequences are so great," said the man.

"So was the disobedience. A line in the universe separates light from darkness. You have crossed that line. You made a tragic choice."

Garden-Maker turned to Woman.

"Why did you eat the fruit?"

"Shining-One said it was good. He told me he'd eaten from it and that it hadn't hurt him."

"Why didn't you ask me?"

"The fruit was beautiful," she cried. "I did not think what looked so good could be so bad. I thought I'd misunderstood the rule of the golden tree."

"Do you understand better now?"

Garden-Maker touched the trembling couple and drew them to himself.

"I love you both very much, but you have eaten the fruit and now the world will change. You have said the consequences are great. You do not know the full truth of your words. All things suffered at your hands." Large, silent tears flowed down the face of Garden-Maker.

"What do you mean?" the woman asked.

"You now know pain and it will not forget you."

Garden-Maker looked deep into her eyes. "Giving birth will no longer be easy. Life will no longer be easy. Your relationship with the man will no longer be easy."

"But I love Man."

"Love will remain, but also conflict. Hateful words and actions will grow from the seeds of selfishness now planted."

Garden-Maker turned to Man. "Woman was tricked, but you made your choice with open eyes. Because of you, Shining-One will wantonly destroy many children. . .your children. And today you and Woman leave the garden. You may no longer eat of its abundance. You must go forth to grow your own food in the land beyond."

Garden-Maker reached deep into his pocket. "Plant, water, and harvest these." Seeds poured into Man's outstretched palms.

"It will not be easy. Even beyond the rivers the land is changed. The goodness in the ground is shriveled. The soil is hard and dry. Thorns and thistles took root and now strangle the beauty of the flowers. Your brow will sweat and your hands will be callused."

Garden-Maker looked away and added solemnly, "Also, you must die." Man and Woman clutched one another's hands.

"To eat from the tree is to die. The poison of the fruit has numbered your heartbeats. Justice requires deaths this morning, but I provide another way."

And Garden-Maker walked toward the stream. They followed along its banks for several minutes until he stopped and pointed to a buck and a doe who lay peacefully but unnaturally by the water.

"Go to them," he ordered.

As they approached, neither animal moved. Suddenly the woman screamed, and the man jumped back. The animals had no breath, and their lifeless eyes stared toward the blue sky.

"What is wrong, Garden-Maker?" cried Man.

"Behold death, the firstfruit of disobedience."

"Why?"

"Justice must be satisfied. Their lives were exchanged for yours and you will live awhile. It gives you many more sunsets but one day you will be as they."

Man and Woman embraced and wept.

"Your time is short," interrupted Garden-Maker. "Skin the deer for your covering, gather what is yours. Bid farewell to the garden. When the sun touches the top of the sky you must leave this place forever."

Suddenly an angel, twice as tall as Man, stood before them. His handsome glowing face was rugged and sensitive. His mouth was grave, while his deep blue eyes twinkled like the stars. A sparkling linen robe hung down to bare feet that seemed to take root into the ground. Gleaming wings were spread as if for flight. Clutched with both hands was the golden hilt of a flaming sword, which he swung back and forth with a speed that human eyes could not follow.

The man and the woman stepped back with mouths open wide.

"This is the guardian of the gate. He will bar the way against all who would return to this paradise."

The man and the woman walked away quietly. As the sun rose in the sky, the man skinned the two deer and made crude clothing while the woman gathered their few belongings. They visited their favorite places and said good-bye to the animals.

They lingered until the sun stood high above, then they stepped from the garden and crossed the river, stepping onto a dry and windswept desert plain. Without looking backward, they walked toward the Mountains of the Dawn. The angel at the eastern gate swung his sword menacingly as the two faded into the distance.

The snake watched with an evil smile. With an arrogant chuckle he slithered past the guarding angel and into the desolate land beyond, always keeping the couple within sight.

UNRESOLVED ANGER AND BITTERNESS
CONSUME LIFE AND SOUL.
THEIR CRUEL INSANITIES
WOULD NOT BE IMAGINED
IN ONE'S RIGHT MIND.

CHAPTER 6

THE BOYS

Screams of pain burst from the rude stone dwelling into the twilight. With every ounce of energy, Woman pushed, biting her lip until it bled. Man wiped the dampness of her brow with his hand.

A tiny head crested, and a hardy male child screamed in lusty rage. Who dared disturb him? Why had he been pulled into this bright and cold and unfriendly place? His cry calmed as he nestled into soft goat's wool and tasted milk. Woman stared into dark eyes and touched tiny fingers as she rocked him.

Garden-Maker had spoken truly—for giving birth was hard and painful. But the pain brought new life and gave new meaning. All that she and Man faced in life faded as Woman cradled her fragile child. Now she took the name of Mother, and many new things filled her days.

First smiles.

First steps.

First words.

And an attitude that reminded Mother and Father of their own childish defiance. They cared for him and protected him and taught him. They told him about the garden and the choices and the exile. Father reminisced about walks with Garden-Maker. Mother warned of the ways of Shining-One. And the boy's black hair grew long and curly. His body became tall and strong. And the defiance of childhood clung to a heart that was stubborn and strong-willed. He was a difficult boy, but his parents loved him as only parents could.

New pain.

New cries.

Another moment of crisis passed.

Now a second son was born. And Mother who had lavished affection on her first son was preoccupied with another. Jealousy and hatred took root in First-Born. The two brothers played together, but the older pushed and harassed and belittled the younger. Second-Born was easy-natured in personality, so he brushed aside the abuse, but became ever more careful around his brother. He tried to make peace with gifts and compliments, but the older brother ignored them. Father and Mother loved both their boys and were saddened by such hostility in their rivalry.

Children became men and grew further and more firmly apart. They rarely spoke and each went his own way.

First-Born cleared the rocks and broke the stubborn soil to sow the seeds his father had received from the hand of Garden-Maker. He turned aside water from a river and dug narrow canals to refresh his crops so that they flourished.

Farther east in the softly rolling hills before the Mountains of the Dawn, Second-Born kept his flocks of sheep. He guided them safely along treacherous paths to green meadows of tall, sweet grass and still, clear waters. He protected them from bears and wolves and eagles.

The voice of Garden-Maker had not been heard since last they stood in the garden. So Man journeyed, walking alone across the windswept desert. He walked toward the setting sun until he came to the rivers and the garden. There he sat, peering past the glowing angel into the alluring perfection of his former home. He recalled the days when he climbed the oak and wrestled with the lion and sat with Woman in fields of fragrant wildflowers. He longed most for his early mornings alone with Garden-Maker.

As he sat in the shadow of the garden, grief overtook him and he cried out:

"Why have you left us all alone?

"We need you!

"I want you! Oh, please talk to me."

The man heard familiar footsteps. A voice echoed and swirled around his head.

"I have waited long to hear you speak, for I also miss our times together," said Garden-Maker.

"But we are exiled from the garden."

"I live beyond the sky, and hold stars in my hands. I know boundaries of neither time nor place. Where you call, there I am."

"I can't see you."

"But I am here as the wind is here. Away from the garden your eyes have grown weak and distorted. Now you see only shadows."

"Though I can't see you, I do feel your presence. The peace is like the serenity of the garden. May I call whenever I wish?"

"Whenever you wish."

As Man walked toward the Mountains of the Dawn he smiled. The best thing of the garden was his. From that day he called on Garden-Maker each morning, and the two of them walked.

He brought Woman and First-Born and Second-Born to the edge of the garden. They stared into the lush setting, awed by its treasured tranquillity. Songbirds chirped an irresistible melody that called the family forward, and a gentle breeze, fresh and sweet and pure, made their mouths water. Unconsciously, their feet drew them closer and closer, until suddenly flames flashed before them, and the angel whose eyes twinkled like the stars blocked their path.

Retreating a safe distance, they sat on the hot sand and looked with longing.

"It's the most beautiful place," exclaimed the younger brother.

"It's not fair!" said the older. "Garden-Maker forced you to leave."

"But we broke the rule of the golden tree."

"It was a small mistake. I thought Garden-Maker had compassion."

"It was a vast mistake, and still he allowed us to live."

"We work like animals and sweat like pigs to survive. In the garden where we belong, life would be easy and everything would be good."

"Life would be perfect," agreed Father, "were it not for choices and consequences."

"You made a choice, not us," the older boy grumbled as he stood. "Why should we suffer for your foolishness?"

"Our choices altered many paths—even for you, whom we love more than life."

"I hate it, I hate Garden-Maker, and I hate you! Why bring us here?

To tease us with what we cannot have because you made mistakes?"

First-Born turned his back on the garden and stomped into the midday heat of the blistering desert.

The man started after him, but his wife called him back. "He is hurt and angry, and he grieves for what he cannot know, as we grieve for what we once knew," she said.

A few days later, the oldest boy came to his mother and father. "I didn't mean it," he said. "I became frustrated and spoke without thinking."

His parents embraced their boy but deep inside they saw the darkness that spread inside First-Born.

Years later, during an early morning talk with Garden-Maker, Man said, "I love to walk with you. We were so foolish to break the rule of the golden tree. But though life is not easy, you allowed us to live. Thank you."

"I am the source of all life," said Garden-Maker.

"I know you need nothing from me," said the man, "but is there anything I can give to you?"

"I want your heart. I long to satisfy the hunger of your soul."

"I do hunger for your presence, and you fill my soul, but I would give more."

"Sacrifice before me a spotless newborn lamb as a symbol of purity and a token of gratitude."

Man and Woman each brought a newborn lamb. The younger brother also carried a lamb. But the older brother brought gifts of his own choosing, bushels of barley and wheat. Garden-Maker joyfully accepted the gifts of Man and Woman and Second-Born, but he did not accept the gifts of First-Born, who again stormed off into the desert.

"Why are you angry?" the voice of Garden-Maker called out.

"You are not fair."

"You knew my requirements, yet you chose another way."

"You accepted my brother's gift."

"He listened and did what I asked," said Garden-Maker.

"It was easy for him. He raises sheep."

"Easy or not, he obeyed. If I had asked for barley and wheat your brother would have brought them. You must move beyond your selfishness."

"No matter how hard I work, you do not appreciate what I do."

"The issue is not what you do, but who you are. Not appreciation, but thankfulness. Not favor but humility."

"I brought my gift, and you rejected it. Go, talk to my brother if he is such a good listener."

"Control your anger or it will destroy you."

"I want no more advice."

Anger did not subside; it burned hotter. At night sleep was replaced with thoughts of past grievances, and consuming hatred. As First-Born chopped and pulled at weeds, a plan formed. He considered every angle: It was so treacherous and brutal that he almost abandoned the scheme. Then his hatred swelled and proved stronger than his scruples.

On a cloudy morning the older brother hiked across the valley floor to the eastern hills. He searched the countryside for his brother's flocks and at sunset spotted specks of white on the brown hills to the south. First-Born scrambled over the rocky ground and greeted his brother with a smile. Second-Born was doubtful of the friendly embrace, but he had hoped for heart changes and an end to enmity.

"It is good to see you," said the younger brother. "What brings you so far?"

"I came to see you."

"You've never wanted to see me before."

"It's time that changed. Come down to the valley for a harvest feast. My fields have yielded better than ever before, and I want to celebrate with my brother."

The two sat around a small campfire of twisted juniper wood and talked into the night. Early the next morning First-Born returned to his farm, sure that his plan would succeed. Before many days, Second-Born followed. A large table was spread at his brother's valley home with more food than Second-Born had ever seen.

There were beans and lentils.

There were fruits and vegetables.

There were breads and wine.

The two ate and slept and ate again. "This has been a great time," the younger brother said on the morning of the fourth day, "but I must return to my flocks. Thank you for your hospitality. Next month I'll have a feast, though it won't be so lavish as yours."

"Before you go let me show you my farm."

First-Born showed his brother the storehouses and the canals. He took him through the orchards and out into the freshly cut wheat fields.

"You've done well with this land," the younger brother said as he walked ahead. "Your fields are beautiful."

"Thank you," First-Born said, as he wrapped his strong, callused hands around the younger one's neck and squeezed.

Second-Born gasped and turned ashen and clawed at his arms. Twisting to look into his older brother's face, Second-Born saw fierce joy and passionate hatred and the shadow of Shining-One. First-Born pressed his hands more tightly together and shook his brother's neck with a violent vigor. Finally the youngest struggled no more, his body fell limp, and his eyes lost focus.

But First-Born would not stop. He gripped the neck even tighter and pounded the lifeless head on a rock until its blood soaked the earth.

Then he dragged his brother to a shallow grave, covered the remains with loose soil, and packed it firm. As the sun beat hot on his back and sweat ran down his face, First-Born scattered wheat chaff and stubble to conceal the burial place.

He washed his face and hands and went about his daily chores.

HATRED MARKS ONE'S FACE,
AND ALIENATES ITS VICTIMS
FROM THOSE THEY LOVE THE MOST.

CHAPTER 7

THE OUTLAW

First-Born stirred morning porridge over an open fire beside his simple clay house. A strong gust of wind swept across the valley floor, shaking the dwelling and First-Born. In the wind was a familiar voice.

"Where is your brother?" asked Garden-Maker.

"How would I know?" replied First-Born, covering the tremble in his voice with a tone of irritation. "If you are concerned, then go look after him."

"He has called out to me through the night," said Garden-Maker.

"What did he say?" asked First-Born. He sat down, for his legs no longer held up his quaking body.

"Listen for yourself," whispered Garden-Maker.

On the wind came a mournful wail. Its haunting melody crept across the land and drew the older brother under its hypnotic power. His ears absorbed the sad notes, and his mind was entranced. Against his will he stood and slowly, cautiously, fearfully followed the echo into the fields.

Its beat became more urgent.

Its melody tore at the soul.

Its crescendo nearly drowned out the wind itself.

First-Born found himself standing on a place where the soil seemed well-trod. The covering of wheat stalks and chaff was swept clean with a gust.

Now the wail deafened. First-Born shook himself free of the trance, plugged his ears and screamed, "He's dead! I know he's dead!" He kicked at the earth under his sandals. "This cannot be!" His eyes darted back and forth in crazed panic. Sweat bathed his face. His heart pounded so hard his chest hurt.

Suddenly the ground itself moved. First-Born screamed and fled in blind, witless terror across the plain. He ran on and on and on, until his sides felt they would burst and his lungs wheezed. On and on and on fear drove him, though the sky itself seemed to pursue. Finally he collapsed, gasping, beside a small spring. He could only crawl to the water's edge and cup his hands for a soothing drink. The liquid splashing on his face refreshed and he fell onto his back, so relieved to be alone.

Away from the wind.

Away from the baleful voice and moving earth.

Away from Garden-Maker. Yes, especially that.

Yet, barely discernible, there it still was, a distant sound like that of his brother's muffled moan. No, it was his thoughts. He relaxed once more, until a voice filled the sky.

"Where is your brother?"

"I do not know," he screamed, turning to face the voice of Garden-Maker. "I have done nothing."

"Why are you running?"

"The wail. . .the horrible voice of grief and pain."

"Your brother cries from his grave," Garden-Maker said calmly.

"I don't know what you're talking about."

First-Born turned away from Garden-Maker. But the wind resumed in fury now, and the mournful lament became louder, . . . ever louder, . . . unbearably louder.

"Why do you play with me!? You know what I've done."

"It happened in my presence. You made me watch your awful act and your pitiful attempt to hide it from my eyes. And even now you will not own your guilt?"

"I. . .I killed Second-Born. I lured him to my field and forced the life from his body with my hands."

The wail stopped.

The wind stilled.

There was silence, absolute silence for many minutes before Garden-Maker spoke.

"You refused to heed me, First-Born. You wouldn't control your anger, so you turned your mind to the will of the one who hates all things. Your bitterness broke you, and then your brother. Now, twisted, broken man, you must bear the consequences of your choices."

The voice of Garden-Maker was drifting away. He seemed to be turning his back to leave.

"Wait, Garden-Maker! You must tell my punishment. What are these consequences?" First-Born chased after the drifting voice.

Then he stopped and fell on his face, for Garden-Maker's eyes could suddenly be viewed. Pools of dazzling flame burned away pretense and plea.

"You have fled your land, and you will not return. Today you became an outlaw,

"without a home,

"without parents,

"without inheritance.

"What you have done will be published throughout the land. Henceforth you are not First-Born, but Outlaw. Your name is that of murderer and hater and fugitive; all who know you will turn their backs, as you turned away from me."

First-Born rose to his knees to beg. "But when it is known, my brother's avengers will seek me out."

"No one will kill you. You will run only from yourself."

"How will you stop them?"

The finger of Garden-Maker scooped a bit of soft, wet dirt from the spring. On Outlaw's cheek he drew crossed lines, one vertical, one horizontal. The finger burned into the flesh and the man cringed in pain, but he stood firm.

"This mark is your protection," Garden-Maker said. "Who harms you must answer to me. Go and do not turn back."

So Outlaw walked east. The sun beat down. The cheek throbbed until it scarred over. He walked until nightfall and the next day walked again. Day after day he wandered through a hot, dry wilderness, avoiding people and struggling to survive. When he no longer could abide his loneliness, he found a secluded valley, far away in the hill country. He married there and built simple huts of sunbaked clay. He cleared the rocks and tilled the poor soil, providing wheat and vegetables to sustain life. Children were born. Other outcasts wandered into the valley, and built houses. But always Outlaw's thoughts were twisted with bitterness and guilt and fear. He enclosed the houses in a thick clay wall to keep out the enemies who would come, for he did not trust the word of Garden-Maker.

By the time of Outlaw's great-great-grandchildren, his people filled the valley.

Some lived in tents and raised cattle.

Some worked metal, forging bronze and iron.

Some farmed like Outlaw, tilling the fields by day but returning to the protection of the walls by night.

The valley thrived, but the people maintained the ways of Outlaw. They were stubborn and hot-tempered and distrustful. They hurt one another with selfish demands. They resented Garden-Maker for making their ancestor an outcast.

So they remained outlaws themselves, following the ways of Shining-One along paths that led to anarchy.

SOME ROADS ARE LONGER AND HARDER
AND LESS TRAVELED THAN OTHERS,
BUT THESE LONELY PATHS FORCE US HIGHER
TO TRANSCEND OUR LIMITATIONS.

CHAPTER 8

THE WALKER

Woman wept uncontrollably. Man comforted her, but nothing could lift the ache from her heart. He held her close, and she buried her head in his shoulder as they stood by a grave in a field of wheat stubble.

"How could he do it?

"What could we have done?

"Where did we go wrong?"

There were no answers to the first questions. They knew well the answer to the last. Slowly, painfully, the two made their way across the field and through the open door into First-Born's house. The woman ran her fingers over the coarse fabric of her oldest son's woolen coat. Man grasped the long shepherd's staff of Second-Born from a corner of the room. The couple sat at a table still littered with remains of the feast of reconciliation. Their sorrow echoed off the empty walls and pulled them back into each other's arms.

Nine cycles of the moon later woman gave birth to a third son. Once again she rocked her infant, once again sang a tiny one to sleep. Man stood close and smiled at this innocent who knew nothing of the pain of life and had not yet heard the seductions of Shining-One.

Childish laughter came to fill the empty void.

The scars faded but did not disappear.

The third son grew into a kind and gentle spirit.

Third-Born took his brother's flocks and each year offered a spotless lamb to Garden-Maker. Often the sun broke over the Mountains of the Dawn to find Man and his son with Garden-Maker. The three of them walked and talked, and all the world seemed at peace.

Man watched Third-Born mature and marry. Sons and daughters were born, who soon had sons and daughters. Centuries passed and when the time was right Walker was born. Walker was Man's favorite, of his many descendants. He seemed different from the beginning.

His eyes were brighter and

his questions deeper and

his heart bigger than those of the other children.

Man knew Walker would sing the songs of Garden-Maker. At six Walker sat beside the most elder of all elders and listened as Man described the garden. He learned about Woman and Shining-One, the choice and the exile. He learned how First-Born's anger grew into the murder of Second-Born. He could see how anger continued to wear sores in the hearts of people.

Walker listened to every word. He thought about the stories and their meanings. Then at age ten he approached Man.

"In all the world one gift would brighten my face above all others."

"And what would that be?" asked Man.

"That someday I would be allowed to walk the morning way with you and Garden-Maker."

"If this is truly your desire," said Man, "then tomorrow it shall be granted. But time with Garden-Maker is not always easy. Though I am a very old man, I get up early and we often walk far. Your legs are young."

"My legs are strong, and my desire to walk stronger."

So Walker joined Man and Garden-Maker every morning, and he soon shared a bond with them that the people of the valley never understood.

"May we walk to the garden?" the boy asked Garden-Maker one morning, just before the sun crested the mountains.

"You may, but neither you nor Man will enter."

"I know," said Walker. "I want to see its beauty."

So Man and Walker and Garden-Maker traveled three days toward the setting sun until they came to the sparkling oasis of the rivers in the midst of the desolate lands. Palms and willows and the branches of a stately oak could be seen swaying with the gentle afternoon breeze. The garden was bright and healthy, draped in every shade of green. A hedge of laurel and wild roses encircled paradise. At the only break in the hedge stood the guardian of the gate with his large shiny wings and his swinging sword of flame.

The three stood silent. Walker stared at the lush verdant garden, staggered by its perfection; Man gazed with longing for the first days. What if different choices had been made, not just for his sake and Woman's, but for all his children?

"Why do not all people come to see this sight? No one would ever follow Shining-One again."

"People pass this way," Man explained, "but their eyes are blinded by Shining-One. They no longer see clearly; their eyes know only shadows and illusions. I try to tell them of the Garden but they do not hear. They whisper behind my back that I am useless and confused and live too much in the old stories. Is that not so?"

It was. People laughed at the stories of Man. Walker had hoped Man did not know of their disrespect. But he did know and was sad and feared for the people.

Garden-Maker walked to the hedge, picked a deep-red rose and handed it to his young companion-traveler. The bloom was flawless, with vivid, velvet petals and a sweet fragrance that replaced all sorrows with joy.

"Breathe deeply the scent of eternity," said Garden-Maker. "These roses will never wilt. I gave a bloom to Man many centuries ago, and its color and scent have not faded. Whenever you smell the bloom you will know the garden."

Walker married; he had sons and daughters, who had sons and daughters. His rose never faded and its fragrance stayed as sweet as the day it was picked. Walker showed it to many as proof of the garden and the Garden-Maker, but only a few saw the depth of its beauty and fewer smelled the scent of eternity.

But Man and Walker spoke many times about that visit to the garden and they dreamed of strolling among the lilies on the banks of the crystal stream of paradise. Every morning the two rubbed slumber from their vision and walked with Garden-Maker, one thousand mornings and ten thousand mornings and one hundred thousand mornings passed, yet the three never missed a dawn together.

Finally, on one spring day, the sun pushed over the mountains and the birds sang their wake-up songs and only two stood at the meeting place.

Walker stared at Garden-Maker with perplexity and panic. Garden-Maker looked back with loving understanding. He touched Walker's shoulder and said, "Go to him."

Walker ran to Man's small dwelling and found him lying on his bed, a light wool blanket pulled tight around his shoulders. His face was gray and his breathing shallow. Walker shook him and cried, "Wake up. Please, wake up and walk with us."

Man slowly opened his eyes, cloudy and unfocused. He tried to rise but collapsed in a fit of ragged coughing and choking. Walker sat on the simple bed and raised Man and patted his back until the choking stopped. Man grasped Walker's arm, his grip weak and shaky.

"The rose," came Man's rough whisper.

"Just rest. You will be all right."

"I know." Man's gasps made every word a struggle. "The rose. On the table."

Walker got the rose and held its soft petals close to Man's face. "Can you smell it?" he asked.

"The garden," Man whispered with a faint smile. "So beautiful. . . If only. . ."

Man's grip relaxed. The rose fell to the floor, though not a petal came loose from the stem. Walker hugged the man, pressing their bodies close, as if his warmth might rekindle life's spark. He sobbed until his chest hurt. Then he lay Man's empty body back on the bed and pressed his wrinkled eyelids shut. He retrieved the rose from the dusty floor and breathed deep. Yes, it did smell of the garden, the scent of eternity.

"Breathe deeply now, first father," he quietly said and left the room.

Men and women gathered outside the garden to bury the man beside the woman. There had been complaints about taking him so far. Why bury Man in such a forsaken wilderness? They looked strangely at Walker when he described the garden's entrance and the shining guardian whose sword he could see swinging to and fro.

Man and Walker, good men.

But they said such odd things.

Must be the walking that causes it.

The keeper of records chiseled a simple epitaph on a rough gray stone over the freshly turned earth:

Man

The Father of Us All.

He Loved Garden-Maker.

The people bowed their heads and wept, for Man and for themselves. They could not catch the scent of eternity on the breeze.

Walker and Garden-Maker met shortly before dawn. Twenty thousand mornings more they walked and talked. Each day the walks journeyed a little farther and the talks ventured a little deeper. They walked until the sun touched the top of the sky, walked until the sun cast long thin shadows over the desert, walked until the moon painted the land with bluish hues.

One morning Walker went out and never returned. The people looked, but he had simply vanished.

Wild animals had eaten him.

No, he was washed away by a river.

No, he had fallen in the desert by his imaginary garden.

But some who really knew him, who had smelled the scent of eternity, insisted that Walker and Garden-Maker had journeyed to the very gate of Garden-Maker's home. It seemed only right that Walker should enter and sit with Garden-Maker and Man and Woman.

Such friends could walk and talk forever.

HARD WORK AND CAREFUL CRAFTSMANSHIP
TURN COMMON LABOR INTO
UNCOMMON DEVOTION—
SHAPING THE SOUL, AND LIFE.

꩜

CHAPTER 9

THE BUILDER

The walker is a myth," laughed the man from the hills.

"Walker lived," answered Builder. "I know he walked with Man. I am sure he knew Garden-Maker."

"Man?"

"Garden-Maker?"

The hill man and his companions shook with mirth.

"If you tell these stories as if you believe," said a kindly hearer, "you will be called a demented fool. You will seem deranged and a danger to sane society.

"Valley mythmakers dreamed such things. It was their pleasure to see meaning and order in the anarchy of life. We are not children, as they."

"You are the mythmakers," said Builder, who turned away toward his mallet and lumber and lathe.

Walker had journeyed away before Builder was born, but Grandfather had known him well. Grandfather, the old one, was Walker's son and spoke of his father's walks with Garden-Maker in the dawn. The old one wouldn't lie, and Builder loved the stories and listened long and yearned to know the truths of Garden-Maker.

The old one was tall and thin and fragile. But he was strong of face and his deep, piercing eyes still shined clear above a beard that had not known a razor for at least one hundred summers. Builder was short and robust, with a smile always close to his lips. The two were an odd pair as they talked in the shade of a willow at the end of the working day.

"Why do people of the hills disbelieve Garden-Maker?" asked Builder.

"They are dark in heart like First-Born, who turned his back on Garden-Maker and became Outlaw. His descendants follow Shining-One, deceived by his lies. Now he twists the children of Second-Born and Third-Born. Few smell the scent of eternity when we hold the ancient rose."

"That is tragic."

"Tragic for us all," said the old one.

"Where does Garden-Maker live?"

"Beyond the sky and beyond time."

"How does one meet someone so far away?"

"He lives far away, but he is not far at all," said the old one. "When you turn, he is there."

"Then how does one walk with him?"

"One has to get up before the sun and go where he leads."

"That sounds easy."

"Not easy," responded the old one, shaking his head. "He doesn't keep to main roads. He takes narrow footpaths over rough ground, where brambles and underbrush obscure the way."

Builder pondered these things as he squared a handsome piece of oak into a simple table. He was a builder, a craftsman, a worker of wood. He knew about walking, for he traveled many miles to search out the best trees.

He liked the giant cyprus and the majestic cedars for size, but the oak had character, and the soft pines had long, clean trunks. The slender boxwood was hard and could be polished until it glowed.

Each wood had its own coloring.

Each grain had its characteristic hardness.

Each tree family could be recognized by smell.

He chopped down his selections and hauled them to his shop where he meticulously cut and carved them into sturdy doors and ornate tables and perfectly balanced wheels. His work was useful and beautiful. People trusted Builder and respected his craftsmanship.

Builder enjoyed the feel of wood in his hands but he wanted something more. Talks with Grandfather strengthened a cherished hope that life was greater and deeper and lovelier than he had seen. Early one morning, before the sun cracked the dawn, Builder rose from his warm bed to search for Garden-Maker.

He scanned the horizon, yet could not find Garden-Maker.

He walked into the desert, but Garden-Maker was not there.

Neither could he be found in the rolling hills.

Builder followed a cascading stream back into the valley, but still no Garden-Maker. Finally, the builder sat down by the side of the road, looked up to the sky, and cried, "Where are you?"

"I am here."

"I've searched for you all morning but couldn't find you."

"Everywhere you went, I was."

"Then why was it so hard?"

"It is not hard to find me, only to follow me."

"So how do I follow you?"

"Meet me here tomorrow morning."

The next morning the two met and walked the great primeval forests north of the valley. Soon a tradition of greeting the day together was established. Side by side the seeker and the Source journeyed the footpaths of the valley and beyond.

One day they walked farther than ever before. When the sun set they were still walking, and when it rose again they continued with their backs to the dawn. After three days the builder stopped and then broke into a full run, sprinting from the riverbank to the fringes of the luscious garden.

He abruptly halted, face-to-face with the guardian of the gate and his flaming sword. He yelled at the top of his lungs, "It's all true. All the old stories are true. Now I've seen it with my own eyes."

"Go tell the others."

"But they won't believe me."

"No, they won't believe you," said Garden-Maker. "I still want you to tell them."

Builder told everybody he met, people from the valley and people in the hills, about the beauty of the garden. They all laughed; each one scoffed, "Prove it."

"Travel three days toward the setting sun and see for yourselves."

They laughed again and went their ways with hearts hard and cold and dark.

Builder watched them go.

He watched them like he'd never watched before.

He watched the people with deepening compassion.

He studied their ways and saw them through the eyes of Garden-Maker's love.

He felt anger as two boys beat an old man, stripping away his coat and pilfering a few silver coins from his bag. Builder chased away the boys and helped the bleeding man to stand.

He felt sorrow as a husband cursed his wife, then struck her with a heavy walking stick until she screamed in pain and terror. Builder tore the stick from the red-faced man. "What are you doing?" Builder implored. "Don't treat her like that!" But the husband shoved Builder down, retrieved his club, and bludgeoned his wife until blood flowed from her skull and her body lay still.

Builder knelt at her side.

He lifted her broken head.

He wept bitterly.

From his home beyond the sky and beyond time, Garden-Maker looked down and saw it all. Tears formed in ageless eyes and he wept with Builder.

COURAGE IS STANDING FIRM
FOR WHAT WE BELIEVE IS RIGHT,
REGARDLESS OF REJECTION AND RIDICULE.

CHAPTER 10

THE BOAT

If a small child is bitten on the heel by a snake," mused Garden-Maker one morning, "and the venom mingles with the blood and flows up the ankle and past the knee—should a loving father cut off the leg to save the life?"

"A father does what he must, however drastic it may seem, to save his child," answered Builder.

"Yes, love sometimes makes severe choices," said Garden-Maker, "so now you must build a boat."

"A boat?"

"Larger than any the blue planet has ever seen—three houses high and spacious enough to shelter a sampling of every animal that roams the land or flies the skies."

"But that is much too big even to float in all the four rivers together, and those rivers are days away."

"Yet you must build, because I love my child. Shining-One has bitten the heel of my creation, and his poison spreads. People are so selfish and violent and brutal that I must send a flood to wash away the poison. So you must build, and I will save you and your wife and your children."

"But I don't have any children."

"You will," the Garden-Maker said with a knowing smile.

"What about my father and father's father?"

"I'll hold back the rains until they walk beyond the lands of the blue planet."

"What will happen to everybody else?"

"The boat will shelter all who are willing. So build the boat and tell the old stories and invite them to safety."

Builder sharpened a stick. He drew lines on the dry ground and considered dimensions and scratched his head doubtfully. Even a simple design would take many years to build. It would take more trees than he could imagine. He kicked away the calculations with his sandal. Who could make such a thing? Builder shook his head and showed his drawings to the old one.

"Is this possible?"

The old man stared at the lines and studied the angles. "Garden-Maker gives impossible tasks. Then he lifts minds and enlarges goals and defeats doubts. In such ways he overcomes every impossibility."

Builder hired men to travel north to a grove of cypress and cut the tallest trees. Many days they split the logs. They fashioned the skids and their oxen slowly pulled the timbers home. People watched their procession, for never had so many trees been felled; never so much been moved at one time.

Builder cut.

Builder shaped and smoothed.

Builder seasoned the fragrant planks and beams.

Years and many trips to the grove were made to cut the needed lumber. He would have given up, but he was sustained by the morning walks with Garden-Maker, though he sometimes felt too tired and sore for them. Garden-Maker encouraged the progress, and shared with Builder his great knowledge in the making of many things.

In time, Garden-Maker sent to Builder a wife who did not laugh or complain about the wood stacked high about the house. Three sons were born.

The first had skin pale like the lily.

The second had skin dark as the obsidian.

The third had skin yellow like the sun.

When the boys grew old enough they helped their father fit the boards tightly to form the hull. People gathered to watch Builder and his three sons cut and hammer.

"You are crazy," someone always yelled.

"It's ridiculous," someone else always said, looking up at the superstructure that towered over the valley floor.

"It looks more like a box than a boat."

"It's too heavy. It will never float."

"Of course it won't float. You need water to float and there's not enough water around here to hold something a fraction that size."

The crowd always laughed and they laughed more derisively as Builder stopped to tell the stories of Garden-Maker and Man and Walker. To the pounding of the sons' hammers, Builder warned of Shining-One's poison and Garden-Maker's sorrow. He told why they built their boat in a dry valley. That brought gales of laughter and abuse, until the people drifted away. But they always returned another day with others to repeat the scene.

Year by year.

Decade after decade.

From generation to generation, Builder told the stories and built the boat, but in all those years only three young women showed interest in picking up hammers and rising before the dawn and walking with Garden-Maker. Only three willingly took Builder's sons as husbands and stood against their parents and abandoned their friends to join the crazy boatbuilders.

Even impossible tasks come to completion when Garden-Maker takes a hand in them. Builder heated pitch in large earthenware pots above open fires. His sons spread the tar to seal each seam. Now they waited, as the crowds grew larger and their taunts more vicious.

Some tried to damage the boat.

Some threw stones at the workers.

All cursed the name of Garden-Maker.

The crowds were quieter when the first creatures arrived, some so strange that none knew what they could be. The sons traveled far beyond the valley and gathered many animals that roamed the earth. People stared as a dusty menagerie paraded across the sunbaked ground.

Flightless birds and soaring reptiles.

White bears and brown bears and black bears.

Miniature monkeys and giant gorillas, panthers and pythons and peacocks.

When each animal had found its stall, everything was ready. The boat was built, the animals gathered, the food stored. The only lack was water, lots of water, more water than the valley had ever known.

Five summers had passed since his father had left the blue planet and now his grandfather lay near death. Builder combed the ancient unkempt beard, squeezed his feeble hand, and said good-bye.

The old one was not sad. His days were more than those of any other on the blue planet. He had watched the world grow violent and vicious and cruel. Now he wanted the peace that only Garden-Maker could give. A strong cool wind howled around the house. The old man's eyes focused, and he sniffed the scent of rain. Through the doorway he could see thick, ominous storm clouds, darker and more dense than ever he had seen. Large drops splattered the ground.

"It is time," said Builder.

The old one nodded and closed his eyes. His hands went limp. Builder kissed his cheek and moved swiftly out into the gathering storm.

Garden-Maker would bury Grandfather.

> THE COLORS OF NATURE
> HOLD ETERNAL MESSAGES
> THAT MOST OF US RARELY
> TAKE THE TIME TO READ.

CHAPTER 11

THE RAINBOW

Driving rain pounded the earth with relentless fury. It soaked the dry ground, then ran down hills into swelling streams that gushed down steep ravines to wash the valley. Black clouds linked horizons, blocking hint of sun and stars and sky. Midday was as midnight. Rivers doubled, then tripled, spilling over the farmlands.

Refugees carrying bags of possessions slogged the mud toward higher ground. Not for a moment did the torrent relent. Soaked and shivering people abandoned their belongings and scrambled for protection. Swift currents crumbled buildings and tore away trees by their roots.

Day followed day without notice in the darkness. Waters rose until the boat jostled its supports. Finally it gently broke free and drifted with the flows. The valley floor was covered with water, yet still the rains came.

Everything was gone—houses, people, livestock. Builder wondered whether waters would reach the garden and cover the guardian of the gate. He tried not to think of those he had known, who were climbing hills until the hills were swallowed, who had scaled mountains until they were washed away.

When the rains stopped, no land was in sight. A few frantic rafters who had lashed together logs to save themselves from the torrent pounded on the hull asking for refuge. When this was refused they begged, "Food. Please give us food and drink." Builder hesitated, then lowered a basket of bread and vegetables and a skin of water. The rafters devoured it and paddled into the distance in search of land.

The boat bobbed and swayed on the open sea. Builder and his family struggled to feed the animals in the misery of their sickness at the continual motion. Life was busy, but tasks were carefully organized:

Each morning and evening the animals were fed and watered.

Every afternoon stalls were cleaned as cows and goats were milked.

Once a week the larger animals were groomed.

The sons and their wives worked hard without complaint. There were tensions as people shared their living space with chimpanzees and camels and crocodiles but disputes were settled quickly. Animals mostly lay about in semisleep. Builder maintained the boat, searching for leaks and making repairs. Builder's wife fixed food, offered encouragement, and watched for a break in the sky.

Finally the rain stopped and the wind died and a calmness spread over the waves. Builder scanned the horizon. All was water, in every direction. Even the snowcapped peaks of the Mountains of the Dawn were submerged. For five cycles of the moon the boat floated at the mercy of current and breeze. Builder's family cared for the animals in an unvarying routine.

Then late one night a crash reverberated through the boat. Builder's eyes jerked open and he flew out of bed. The awful noise continued as something scraped pitch and strained boards.

"To the lower deck," he yelled. "We have to reinforce the hull before it rips open."

Torch-illuminated men and women raced down the stairs as Builder grabbed lumber and mallets. The scraping continued—a long, rough screeching of wood against stone. Suddenly the boat lurched to a stop. It groaned and strained but did not move.

"There is a breach," a voice called out. Builder rushed to the tear as water burst through a hole in the splintered wood about the size of a small child. Animals yelped and bellowed as the sea poured around them. One man forced boards over the open wound while the other two pounded them into place. The water slowed to a trickle and the animals quieted. Heated by torches, thick tar seeped into the rift until the bubbling water subsided. Bucket by bucket, the water was raised by rope and dumped overboard in the darkness.

At first light they searched the horizon, but no land could be seen.

"We rest on a mountaintop," said Builder. "Surely the water ebbs, and soon we will see land."

Each morning the family hoped for a hint of dry ground. But it was more than two moon cycles later that Builder cried out, "There it is! Land! I see it!"

Small rock islands were anchored in the sea's vast flatness. Precious stores opened that night for a feast, with meat and cakes and plenty of red wine.

"If only we could free ourselves from these rocks," reasoned a son, "we could drift over to the islands and get off this boat."

"The risk of damage is too great," Builder warned. "We'd tear more holes in the hull. Be patient. The water is receding and soon we will stand on dry land."

Each day the islands grew bigger and the passengers of the boat more impatient. Finally Builder said, "Let's send out a dove. If it returns, we will know the islands can't support life. If it doesn't return, we'll know it is time to open the doors and leave."

Just before the sun touched the roof of the sky, a single gray and white dove was released with a prayer to Garden-Maker. Sixteen eyes watched the dove fly toward the islands and then disappear in the distance. But soon the bird reappeared in the open window, and that night the family ate in silence.

Seven endless days dragged by before the dove was loosed again.

"It's spring and the islands grow larger daily. Maybe this time the bird will find a home."

Hours slipped by, and the dove didn't return. A strained excitement rose when mealtime came and went. Eight souls gathered to watch the last long rays of the sun glitter on the waves of the deep.

Suddenly the dove appeared and perched on the builder's hand, a small green leaf clutched in its hard beak. Everyone sighed, except Builder. He reached out and took the leaf. "New growth from an olive tree," he said. "Garden-Maker has sent a great sign."

"But the bird came back," said one son with the hint of a scowl.

"Next time it will not," Builder promised. "The hardy olive tree grows high on the mountain. If it sprouts growth, other foliage will not lag far behind."

Seven days later the dove lifted into the sunrise. By the sun's setting the bird had not returned. The sea grew dark and Builder lit torches to guide the dove's return, but it was gone. More torches were lit for a festival. Eight sea-weary boaters sang and danced under a star-studded sky until the sun again peeked through the half-submerged Mountains of the Dawn.

Builder and his sons opened the doors and let the animals free into a bright morning aglow with spring. It was a scene of peace invaded by chaos as hundreds of birds and insects stretched their wings in thunderous applause; mammals galloped, hopped, lumbered and stampeded down the bridge from ship to soil; reptiles and amphibians slid and slithered and dived into a new world. Eight travelers on an abandoned ship gathered their belongings and considered their future.

"First we must thank Garden-Maker," said Builder.

"Thank him for flooding the earth?" asked one of his sons.

"Thank him for saving us."

"The boat saved us and we built the boat."

"Garden-Maker told us what to do. His hand strengthened our hands. His love cleansed evil from the blue planet. We must never forget Garden-Maker and all he has done for us."

The next day Builder piled stone upon stone to form an altar on the mountain plateau. On one side lay the grounded boat, on the other the drowned world. In the fire atop the stones, Builder sacrificed a newborn lamb and a pair of young doves. The twisted juniper branches sizzled with the water still soaked inside, then crackled, then burst into bright orange arms, engulfing the sacrifice.

Flames danced and leaped joyfully above the wood and stones.

Waves of heat drove Builder back.

Gray transparent smoke rose to the sky and beyond.

Garden-Maker smiled and said to his angels, "They have not forgotten me." In a moment he stood near Builder. "Thank you for your token of gratitude."

"We owe all to you who have saved us."

"I give you a solemn promise," said Garden-Maker. "Only once will I send the flood upon the blue planet. Never again will waters cover the Mountains of the Dawn. I love you and your family. I love your future children and their children's children. From now on when sun and water mingle above the earth, a banner of light will stretch across the sky. Tell your descendants that when they see my banner they should remember that, no matter how distant I seem, I am always close and I will always care."

A drop of rain gently splashed on Builder's face, and he looked up to see the sun shine through a storm cloud. Across the sky a bow of vivid reds and yellows and blues arched above the earth, its ends lost in distant hills. Builder stared at the beautiful symbol of Garden-Maker's promise.

"Now we begin once more," he said to himself. "With Garden-Maker's help, perhaps we can do it right this time." He watched the rainbow fade into sun.

Meanwhile, an ancient snake with devious eyes watched from behind the rocks near the altar and shook its shiny head.

BUILDING MONUMENTS IS A WASTE OF TIME
UNLESS THEY SERVE AS STEADY SIGNPOSTS
TOWARD ETERNAL VALUES.

CHAPTER 12

THE GATEWAY TO HEAVEN

Builder sat in the shadow of the boat and watched the sun beat down on the valley below where a river meandered toward the southern sea. His sons plowed a fresh field in the fertile silt left by the flood and dropped seeds into the narrow furrows. A cool breeze blew down over the mountaintop and Builder felt the presence of Garden-Maker.

The next day Builder selected a gently sloping hillside and planted grape cuttings he had saved from his small vineyard before the great rain. In time the vines climbed a simple arbor with their large green leaves and plump, purple grapes hanging in heavy clumps. The builder collected and crushed the grapes, pouring the juice into large clay pots to age. Then he sat in the shade of his arbor and watched the world change.

Houses were built.

Herds of cattle and sheep were raised and fields were tilled.

Grandchildren and great-grandchildren were born.

Builder's descendants spread across the countryside, moving out of the valley and into the land between the four rivers and the Mountains of the Dawn. Yet Builder was not forgotten. His sons came back each year, even after his wife died, and they sat under his arbor listening to the stories of Garden-Maker and Man and Walker, of life before the great rain.

His grandsons and great-grandsons had less respect. They ridiculed Builder and his stories about Garden-Maker. "He's an old man, senile and broken-down," they laughed. "Time with the juice of his grapes confuses him. He makes up stories one minute and believes them the next."

One of the builder's great-grandsons was a hunter. He traveled south in search of fame and founded a small settlement on a wide plain along a

66

river. Hunter was a powerful warrior and a master of the bow. He was a leader prudent and handsome and strong. Problems and disputes were brought to Hunter, who reflected and resolved with a patient wisdom. Hunter's small settlement grew to a village then a large town then a thriving city. Then it was the largest city in all the blue planet.

The city was home to farmers of the plain, to herdsmen whose flocks roamed the nearby hills, to craftsmen who shaped beauty from metal and wood and pottery. In time a thick brick wall surrounded the city. It wasn't that the world had filled with dangers so soon. But their fine wall made people feel safe and snug, and proud that they could make such a thing. Shining-One felt especially happy in such a city, where people trusted a wall above Garden-Maker.

Garden-Maker looked upon the city from his home beyond the sky and shook his head.

No one woke before the sun to walk with him.

No one called his name, even in time of need.

No one offered a sacrifice as a token of gratitude.

Few remembered that every rainbow was a message that he is always close and always cares. Even fewer had heard the old stories of Man and Woman and their choice. Certain wise people feared the ancient tales would be lost forever, so they collected them, wrote them down on clay tablets and stored them in great stone vaults. But even the wise ones viewed the stories as fables and fantasies, wishful thinking of less learned generations who looked for meaning in the meaningless.

Shining-One basked in the afternoon sun just outside the city gates, waiting. The snake followed when Hunter passed by, whispering in his ear: "I live beyond the sky and hold the stars in my hands. I am the ruler of this world and will someday control the entire universe. I am infinite and eternal and all-powerful. I am the morning star, and all the stars of heaven worship me. Follow me, and I will make you great."

"I'm already great," said Hunter. "I have built the largest city of all on the face of the blue planet."

"Cities come and go," hissed Shining-One. "Build me a temple that touches the sky, and I will show you how to read the stars."

"What can stars tell that I don't already know?"

"The stars hold secret wisdom. If you can read the heavens, you can control your destiny and spread your name among all the people of the blue planet."

That afternoon Hunter met with the city leaders and commissioned them to design the tallest, most impressive of structures. "I want it to be a monument to human ingenuity, an observatory of the stars, and a temple to Shining-One," Hunter explained. "It shall be called the Gateway to Heaven and shall guarantee us immortality." This was thought a most wise and worthwhile project. Soon they presented to Hunter plans for an artificial mountain that would rise high above the plain and the rest of the city. It was a breathtaking vision.

"This is incredible!" said Hunter. "How tall will it be?"

"Twice as high as the tallest cedar," said the most distinguished-looking planner.

"How high can you go?" Hunter asked.

"Until you run out of bricks."

It took years to make the bricks. Soft clay of the river was pressed into molds. The rectangular shapes baked in large outside ovens until they glistened like copper. Finally work on the Gateway to Heaven could begin in earnest.

Pallets of bricks were hauled by oxen.

They were lifted by pulley and lever to the workers above.

They were secured in neat rows with thick tar.

The people of the city were hard workers. Keeping them busy kept them quiet and gave them purpose. Success and honor was measured by the number of bricks set into place through each cycle of the moon.

At night the "people of the sky" climbed the temple and sat all night, watching and writing. They divided the heavens to chart the course of stars and plot the paths of planets. Suns and nebula and galaxies and asteroids were all thoughtfully observed. But the moon demanded special attention. They watched it closely and used its turnings to devise a more accurate calendar. The sky was filled with magic and perhaps the universe itself revolved around the marvelous mountain.

The people of the sky became the priests to the temple of Shining-One. City dwellers came to them for advice and guidance. The priests were at first reluctant, but they became confident and then arrogant. They saw every answer written in the sky and each soul reflected in the stars. Stars were linked to become pictures of people and animals. The priests proclaimed these figures as destiny-shapers. Each person in the city took one of these sky figures as a personal guide. One was even called "the hunter" in honor of their leader. But greater than the constellations was Shining-One, the hidden hand that held all stars and the destinies in his hands.

Shining-One finally achieved a hint of the recognition he believed he deserved. Here was his creation and he laughed at how easily the city dwellers could be deceived.

Garden-Maker looked down on the temple and wept. Turning to his angels, he asked, "Why would people believe a lie rather than walk with me?"

Several years later the people of the sky came to the hunter with a plan to enlarge their temple. "If it was taller still we could see more stars. Then we could know all things and the future would be even more clear."

Hunter approved and the expansion began at once. As artisans labored, Garden-Maker tugged on the heart of Hunter, but the city founder ignored his own discomfort. But Garden-Maker was not easily put off. When darkness crept over the city and its people slept inside the false security of the walls and under the false security of the stars, Garden-Maker visited Hunter.

"Come and walk with me."

"What can you give me that I don't already have?"

"Eternity."

"The Gateway to Heaven will give me eternity."

"Your mountain is mud and tar," said Garden-Maker. "It cannot give what you want."

"Shining-One says it will give me knowledge of all things."

"Shining-One says whatever will turn your heart his way. I speak what is true whether you hear it or not. Shining-One deals illusions. Walk with me and you will have more than you could ever imagine—and it will be real."

"And in return?"

"Tear down your temple of illusion," Garden-Maker said calmly.

"The mountain is mine!" Hunter shouted. "It is beautiful—the tallest building on the blue planet. And I am making it even taller."

"It is mud and tar. One strong wind and it is rubble."

"You're just jealous. You know that if the Gateway to Heaven is built higher, I will learn your secrets."

"I am not threatened. I am concerned, for your alliance is with a darkness more menacing than anything your wall can keep out."

"Leave me alone!" screamed Hunter, covering his ears. "I will never tear down my temple and I will never walk with you. Get out of my city and don't return!"

Hunter walked away.

Garden-Maker turned away.

Shining-One smirked.

Early the next morning a vortex spun high above the blue planet. Its whirling wind fell from the sky. Dust choked the air, so thick none of the people could see or breathe. The people of the sky were shaken and blown from their observing places on the artificial mountain. Their screams as they fell from the sky were muffled by the wind and the swirling dust. The earth shook and the mountain swayed. Bricks broke from the higher levels and crashed into the houses of the city. The streets filled with panic and destruction and death as people trampled each other in fleeing the city of falling bricks.

There was shouting and yelling and screaming. The volume increased with voices becoming more frantic and hysterical. It built to a deafening noise surrounding the city and everybody in it. Then the noise split into a hundred different pieces. Strange sounds came from people's mouths. Fear filled their eyes as they could no longer understand their closest friends and neighbors.

Then suddenly the wind was silent.

The earth stopped rumbling.

Bricks no longer rained down from the hideously broken mountain.

But now the people had to search out those whose words were understood. Slowly groups formed among those with a common speech. Inside and outside the walls were small collections of refugees. They trembled in fear. They buried their dead. They gathered a few belongings and turned their backs on their fallen city.

Some crossed the Mountains of the Dawn and settled in the eastern lands; some journeyed across the desert and headed south into the fertile delta that fed the great sea; others went upriver and over the hills to the thick forests of the north; still others stayed in the valley, tilling fields and tending flocks. The city itself was deserted and the mountain gateway abandoned, a curious heap of rubble that passing shepherds looked at in wonder.

Hunter took his bow and set off to found other settlements along the river. Some of these also became great cities, always with high protective walls and elegant temples devoted to Shining-One.

But there were none as great or impressive as the Gateway to Heaven.

ONLY THE FOOLISH AND ARROGANT
HAVE ANSWERS FOR EVERY QUESTION.
THE WISE CRY FOR UNDERSTANDING,
AND ARE CONTENT TO WAIT.

CHAPTER 13

THE LAND-BARON

West of the river, far from the abandoned Gateway to Heaven, lived one of the few people on the blue planet who still walked with Garden-Maker. This man had worked hard to build a large and prosperous farm. Yet he remained quiet and humble, for he knew life's twists and turns. He lived with his wife in a simple house of sunbaked brick in the village. His grown children lived in large stone dwellings in the surrounding hills. Life was good and he was content. His neighbors called him Land-Baron, but he felt that name too ostentatious.

Land-Baron's family was large and tightly knit. His children gathered to celebrate each other's birthdays with extravagant feasts of wine and dancing. After each party Land-Baron would sacrifice ten spotless lambs to Garden-Maker, one for each of his ten children. If only his sons and daughters would walk with Garden-Maker, but they were too busy. So he made sacrifices for them and hoped Garden-Maker would understand. After one sacrifice, a snake slithered from behind the Land-Baron's altar, hissing in disgust.

Shining-One flashed across the universe to a place beyond the sky.

"What maliciousness are you plotting?" asked Garden-Maker.

"I've roamed the blue planet in search of victims but it is all so easy," said Shining-One. "People are weak and pathetic; I whisper, and they do what I wish."

"Not everyone falls so easily."

"Name one who is not soft clay in my hand."

"Have you noticed Land-Baron on your journeys?"

"Yes, but he doesn't count."

"Why not?"

"Everything he touches turns to gold. Sure, he'll walk with you as long as he's one of the wealthiest men in the world. But pressure him and corner him and take his prosperity. Then he'll crack like all others."

"Land-Baron has integrity and depth."

"Let me play with him and you will see what he is."

"Play your little game with Land-Baron's possessions."

Suddenly the universe was silent. Land-Baron studied the late afternoon sky and saw a wall of black clouds moving in. Thunder shook the house. Sudden darkness left Land-Baron stumbling through the dark for an oil lamp. Lightning struck all around. His wife clung to his side, shaking.

"Was ever thunder and lightning so violent. Are we safe?"

"Garden-Maker will protect us."

"How can you be so sure?"

"I've heard the story of Builder. I've seen the banner across the sky, the reminder that Garden-Maker is always close and will always care."

Husband and wife held each other and waited out the storm. Would the fury never stop? Then, just before sunset, the clouds parted.

An urgent knock sounded on Land-Baron's door. An exhausted messenger panted before him, "I'm so sorry," he began. "We were out in the fields plowing, when bandits rode out of the southern deserts. They slaughtered all the oxen and donkeys and farmhands."

Even while he was explaining all this, another man came running up. "I'm so sorry. Lightning struck the pasturelands and started grass fires. We tried to save the sheep, but. . ."

"Sir! Sir!"

A third messenger raced toward the door. "I'm so sorry," he panted. "Three bands of nomadic stargazers drove off your camel herds toward the ruins of the Gateway to Heaven. All the herdsmen were killed except me."

Now a fourth messenger was stumbling up onto the doorstep. "I'm so sorry," he cried with tears running down his dusty cheeks. "All your children were celebrating at your oldest son's home when a powerful wind hit the house. The roof collapsed. Everybody was killed. . . ."

"*Whyyyyyyyyy!*"

The wail echoed through the village. Townspeople came running to see what was wrong, to know why anyone would utter such agony. Land-Baron cried until his throat was raw and his tears spent. Then he bowed to Garden-Maker. "You have given much and now you've taken much. I've lost everything, but I will still walk with you."

Again Shining-One flashed across the universe to Garden-Maker's home.

"What malice are you plotting now?" asked Garden-Maker.

"I roam the blue planet, seeing who I can get to fall."

"Have you considered Land-Baron? He has suffered much, yet he does not stumble."

"He's a stubborn man," hissed Shining-One, "but his heart is as selfish as anyone's. Let me touch his body. A little physical pain, and he will never walk with you again."

"You may touch his body."

Land-Baron's face paled as shooting pains radiated from his chest. He clutched his heart and gasped for breath.

"What's wrong?" his wife ran to his side.

He breathed deeply and the pain subsided. "I don't know, but I have need of rest."

"What's this on your forehead?" asked his wife as she ran her fingers over a swollen purple blotch above his right eyebrow. Over the next few days a raging skin infection spread across his face, breaking out in a series of abscesses and boils. Spongy tumors erupted on his forehead, his nose and his chin. His face swelled until his features were distorted. The disease ate away skin and muscle between the bones of his hands, leaving them deformed. Fever drenched his body with foul sweat.

Land-Baron could find no comfort. When exhaustion overwhelmed him, night terrors taunted his sleep. During the day unrestrained itching left him crazed. His legs grew thick and swollen until his knees and ankles could not be distinguished. His hard skin cracked and ulcerated, seeping onto the strips of cloth that served as bandages.

The stench forced his wife to keep her distance.

Children stared.

Adults turned their eyes away.

Even the village healer held his breath when he examined the wounds. The healer took Land-Baron's wife aside.

"I wish there was something I could give, but I can do nothing even to ease his suffering. We must protect the village from this horrid sickness. Land-Baron must live in isolation outside the village."

"Must I go with him? Why should I have to suffer because of his disease? Why don't his brothers and sisters take care of him?"

"Your husband won't live long. Try to make his final days comfortable."

That afternoon Land-Baron moved outside the village. Every step was painful and not even his wife would touch him to help. But his cracked and bleeding lips never complained. He carried his revolting body with a grace.

"Aren't you angry at Garden-Maker?" His wife spit the words into his face. "Look what you get for all your effort to be his friend and walk with him."

"I didn't walk with Garden-Maker to get anything. I did it because of who he is."

"A liar he is. The sky banner to remind us of his care? Look at what he does to his most faithful. He shouldn't care so much."

"There is a reason for all I don't understand. Garden-Maker has an intent. I know he does."

"You pathetic optimist. Cry out to Garden-Maker until you lose your voice. If I were you, I'd curse his name and die."

Land-Baron was silent as he sat in the dusty heat and gritted his teeth against the torment. His wife shook her head and turned away and walked back toward the village.

Word of the Land-Baron's trauma spread. Three wise men of religion and philosophy traveled to the village to comfort their old friend. They could hardly recognize the shell that groaned in the ash heaps along the road.

His face looked inhuman.

His arms were deformed.

His legs were so swollen and discolored.

The three shocked men broke into uncontrolled tears. They fell to the ground beside their unfortunate friend. Then, because they could think of nothing to say, they simply sat with him.

Finally, Land-Baron broke his silence.

"I can't go on. The pain is overwhelming, but the isolation from Garden-Maker is worse. I long to walk with him, but look at these." He pointed at his distended legs. "I can't even move anymore."

"What has happened to you?" asked one friend.

"I don't know. I wish I'd never been born. My worst nightmare is reality and I have no idea why."

"You have done something serious against Garden-Maker to deserve this," said the friend.

"I cannot think of what. . ."

"Think harder. Your only hope is to admit what you've done and plead for mercy."

"Show me what I've done, and I'll gladly confess it. I would rather repent than know such suffering."

"But Garden-Maker would not have allowed this unless you have done something," broke in another wise man.

"I have been honest and generous and caring. I've loved Garden-Maker and my neighbors. I have lived above reproach. No one has anything against me. Condemn me for something specific, or leave me alone to die in peace."

"Is Garden-Maker then unfair? If you're innocent and ask for his help, it will happen."

"But if it doesn't?"

"Then obviously you are guilty."

"All are guilty," snapped Land-Baron, "but since I was old enough to understand, I have awakened and walked with Garden-Maker. I have tried to follow his ways, no matter how difficult."

"You have not been sincere," suggested the second man.

"I was."

"Maybe that wasn't enough. Have you asked his forgiveness?" asked the third.

"I fell on my face, begging Garden-Maker to forgive me for every hurt or offense."

"You hold a secret vice. Let go of it, and you will prosper again."

Finally Land-Baron exploded.

"You are so arrogant, with all the answers! I don't believe you. Life isn't as neat and simple as you suppose it to be. Sometimes evil triumphs for reasons we will not know. Garden-Maker has his purposes beyond reward or punishment. Maybe his ways are so far beyond our feeble minds that we'll never understand. Return to your pat answers and let me die."

The wise men picked up their staffs and left, muttering about the ungrateful hearts of the wicked. After they left, Land-Baron lay back and closed his eyes and prepared to die.

A dark and powerful storm blew across the countryside. It scooped the ashes from about Land-Baron into a white whirlwind that spun in front of the feeble outcast. He opened his eyes and sat up. From the center of the perfect spiral came a powerful voice.

"I am Garden-Maker. I live beyond the sky and hold the stars in my hands. I am infinite and eternal and all-powerful. No one knows my mind and no one understands my ways. Do you understand how I created the universe? Or how the blue planet revolves around the sun? Or what holds the stars in space? Or why the human mind is able to calculate geometry or learn different languages?"

The Land-Baron shook his head in silence.

"I need you," he pleaded. "Without you I am nothing. I long to walk with you again and see your banner spread across the sky."

"The world is full of things beyond your comprehension. The disease that is eating your flesh has meanings beyond what you and your wise friends and even Shining-One can apprehend."

"Forgive my questioning," said the Land-Baron with his head bent low. "You promised you would always be near and would always care. From this day I believe, whatever I experience. Who am I to judge your workings?"

"You have learned much," said Garden-Maker. "Tomorrow we shall walk."

Suddenly the whirlwind stopped and the storm clouds parted. More wondrous to Land-Baron, his fever broke, and the horrible itching was gone.

A varicolored arch spread across the sky and Land-Baron smiled. He stretched his legs and stood up, for the swelling and discoloration was shrinking before his eyes. By evening his wife dragged the healer out to examine Land-Baron.

"No disease remains in his body," declared the doctor. "There are not even any scars."

That night Land-Baron slept in his own bed beside his most contrite wife. The next morning, after a satisfying walk with Garden-Maker, the village gathered around him to celebrate his recovery.

Land-Baron toasted a new beginning, and Shining-One slithered off into the desert, always in search.

EPILOGUE

Thirteen nights had passed, and thirteen stories had been told. The earliest days of the blue planet had been visited and the image of the Garden-Maker had been revealed. But now the fire burned low. In a little time the dawn would break.

The old man pulled absentmindedly at his gray beard. He slowly stood up, shaking off the chill and soreness. Then he felt the tug on his robe.

"Is it time?"

The one who spoke was a girl child who had not finished her ninth year.

"It is time for young ones to be in bed," he answered kindly.

"No, is it time to walk—to go and walk with Garden-Maker?"

"Yes, Granddaughter, it is time. It is always time for that."

"I also long to walk with Garden-Maker."

The old man looked at the child and saw the tomorrow of the blue planet. He took her hand and turned to face the first hint of light on the horizon.

Hand in hand they began a morning journey.

"Now we meet Garden-Maker," said the man. "Later I will tell you more of his ways."

PART 2
THE PROMISE-KEEPER

TABLE OF CONTENTS
The Promise-Keeper

PROLOGUE

Life was settling in for the night.

It had been a long, hot, hardworking day. Few men gathered, since spring lambs would be born this night, and shepherds would be midwives. Lambs often entered life with such reluctance, as if they were warned away. But all the women and children sat cross-legged around the fire pit. No one wanted to miss listening to the old man with his hundred wrinkles.

Several older women, stoop-shouldered and well-weathered, meticulously set pieces from their precious stock of fig and olive wood branches in the fire pit. They moved with purpose, positioning each piece to send out its best light and heat and fragrant aroma. When all agreed, the oldest of the women ignited twigs and tinder. Seasoned branches crackled and smoked and burst into flame. The circle glowed with new light. How delightful to burn away the chill in the air now that the warmth of the sun was nearly gone. The sky was clear and cloudless. Women chatted and children chattered, but none wandered off to bed or play.

Tonight the storyteller would tell the first of the next seventeen stories—stories about the wise men and stalwart women who first walked paths of a new land. The girl child had heard each before, and she would try hard this night to commit words to memory. She loved these ancient stories of Garden-Maker and how he came to be known as Promise-Keeper.

The old man with the tangled gray beard entered the circle, and the girl child waved timidly. The old man smiled with a warm twinkle in his eyes and continued his steps to the center. He reached into his plain wool robe and threw something into the fire. The flames leaped heavenward with a "whooomp!" and a flash of light that forced everyone to glance away. A blink or two later their eyes readjusted to the ancient figure.

"Are the stories all true?" the girl child whispered to her mother.

"Every one of them," came the confident reply.

With a contented smile she nestled against her mother as the old man cleared his throat.

TRUTH IS USUALLY ONE STEP
BEYOND ONE'S VISION
AND TWO STEPS
BEYOND ONE'S COMFORT.

CHAPTER 1

THE MERCHANT

Follow the truth," she whispered, "wherever it may take you."

The room was deep in shadows as the gray-haired woman on the simple bed closed her eyes and coughed. Her chest heaved, jerking her frail body up and down.

"You'll get better, mother," said her young son. He slipped one small hand behind her neck and brought a clay cup of water to her trembling lips with the other. "You've got to get better."

She sipped the warm water.

The boy stroked her long hair.

She smiled and touched his hand.

"Remember my words," she stressed as she closed her eyes again.

"The stars show you'll be better soon," said the boy. "Father said to always trust the stars."

"Where is your father?" asked the mother.

"Bringing a healer and a priest from the ziggurat."

"Tell him I waited as long as I could." Jagged coughing shook her tired frame one last time. When the healer and the priest arrived there was nothing left to do.

Father hugged his son and they cried. For days the entire city seemed to mourn. The father was a wealthy merchant who traveled the fertile crescent. Both rich and poor knew his fair scales and honest dealings. The wife of such importance was entitled to temple burial honors due royalty. Yet this was a place of business, and by the end of the period of tears, the City of the Moon had long since returned to its busy life.

Tens of thousands bustled about the City of the Moon. Two broad canals circled the town and stretched to the river, while a third cut through the city, separating the temple and businesses from the white lime-washed brick houses and the carefully tended courtyards of the rich. What most fascinated the boy was the canal docks, where foreign vessels traded with local coppersmiths and potters, fishermen and farmers. Colorful and exotic travelers from around the world convened at the marketplace. It was a festive collision of sights and sounds and smells. Buyers and sellers haggled over prices; sheep and cattle complained noisily of their lot in life; stands of fresh fish and ornate jewelry and vivid silks shone in the sun; children raced through the dusty streets, laughing and playing. The place was alive with excitement.

Massive walls ringed the city. Beyond lay a patchwork of cultivated fields laced by irrigation ditches. Above towered the impressive structure of the temple to the moon god. This was not just any temple, but a ziggurat —and a ziggurat as large as twenty houses. It rose high above the temple grounds in three stepped terraces. Not so grand as the ruined Gateway to Heaven, it still was a powerful beacon that could be seen from a long day's journey away. The city was a sanctuary against nomad invaders and safety from the threat of river-plain floods.

But instead of walking with Garden-Maker, the people had been deceived by Shining-One. They prostrated themselves before the moon at the ziggurat they called the "Heavenly Mountain."

The boy's father remarried, to a widowed daughter of the royal family. The father's other sons were much older and had families and their own business interests. The stepmother had different plans for the third son. She presented him at the ziggurat to study as a stargazer. The father agreed. It was good for business to have an intercessor attending the deities of the moon and stars.

The lad learned to trace the lines of the twelve constellations.

He could chart the movement of planets.

His sharp eyes plotted four faint specks of light the priests had not seen.

But the boy sought for more than new stars. Deep inside he heard his mother's words. He must seek truth, and he wondered if there was not someone beyond the sky who held these stars in his hands. He tried to ignore that idea, deep and disturbing, but still the words echoed: "Follow the truth wherever it may take you."

So the young man could not remain a stargazer. He saw no future written in the sky. He found no fates reflected in the stars. He saw only the arrogant priests and the naïve worshipers. So he left the ziggurat to be a merchant as his father and brothers. He met in the marketplace with traders from throughout the world. He watched the ships as they unloaded their goods—

Lumber and silver from the north;

Rare spices and scented woods from the east;

Linen and ivory from the broad river delta to the west;

Gold and pearls and emeralds from the southern desert with its rugged coastline.

He traveled the fertile crescent and then journeyed south into the Land of Deltas where the greatest of all rivers emptied into the Great Sea. There he purchased ebony and copper and frankincense to trade in the City of the Moon. On his journeys Merchant did more than buy and sell. He listened to legends and lore, searching for the truth of one who lived beyond the sky. So he came to hear ancient stories of Man and Woman, of Shining-One and his revolt, of the choice and the exile, of Outlaw and Walker.

Some say Merchant heard the tales directly from Builder as the two sat in the shade of Builder's vineyard arbors. Or perhaps he heard them from the mysterious king in the City of Palms in the high country above the Salty Sea. Whatever their source, these tales of Garden-Maker fascinated Merchant. As he contemplated them, they worked their way deep into his heart.

Merchant did well and he married Princess. She was the most beautiful woman in the City of the Moon and many tried to win her hand. Merchant was handsome with clean-shaven olive skin and long dark hair— parted in the middle and hanging to his shoulders. But it wasn't his beauty that captured her heart. Merchant and Princess had always known one another, for she was the daughter of the merchant's father and stepmother. He had heard her first cries. As a young child she had watched his gentleness and generosity and sensitivity. Most of all she admired his determination to follow the truth. And so she loved and took the hand of her half-brother.

But her marriage was hard, for she could not give a child-heir to carry on the family's name and wealth. She consulted the best healers, taking their herbs and medicines and advice. She spoke to the stargazers and offered sacrifices to the moon god. No child swelled her womb.

Merchant's friends and colleagues ridiculed him and his father questioned his choice of a wife. "My daughter has failed you," his father said. "Leave her and remarry and have a son or all will mock you."

"No, I will love and stay with her to the end," Merchant responded firmly.

Years passed and the merchant's hair turned gray. One afternoon as he rested in the garden by his large house, a warm breeze blew in from the desert. Out of the wind came a strong voice:

"I live beyond the sky and hold the stars in my hands."

The man fell on his face and his heart pounded with joy for he knew he was in the presence of his greatest desire.

"I have heard of you," Merchant began timidly. "You are Garden-Maker?"

"I am. I come to ask a question: Will you follow the truth wherever it may take you?"

"Yes. . .Yes! Oh, you have looked into my heart."

"You believe the stories of me? You hunger to know more?"

"I long to follow the truth. But I do not know how to find it."

"Leave behind your home. Abandon your business. Walk away from the City of the Moon and follow where I lead."

Merchant could make no sense of this. Such a plan was so contrary to the sayings of the moon teachers.

"How can I do something as drastic as this?"

"The beginning of truth is to follow my words even if they seem strange or difficult or confusing. For disaster is about to befall the moon people. Raiders from the Mountains of the Dawn will loot their riches and capture their citizens."

"Where shall I go?"

"Walk with me and I will make you the father of a powerful people."

Father? Were Merchant not so afraid, he would have laughed: "Haven't you heard? My wife and I will never have children."

"Walk with me and I will make you the father of a powerful people," Garden-Maker repeated.

"Where will you take us?"

"Toward truth. Trust me and I will take you to a new land."

"I want to trust. I want to walk with you and follow truth—but leave my life behind?"

"That is how to follow truth. Walk with me."

"How far?"

"Until I stop," whispered the wind. "I know what I ask is neither comfortable nor simple nor safe. For following the truth is not always easy."

The wind calmed.

The voice disappeared.

Merchant stood alone with his quest.

CHAPTER 2

THE CARAVAN

The merchant sat alone in his silent garden, stunned and staring. He had promised his mother to follow the truth wherever it took him. But truth had led to one who lived beyond the sky, who held the stars in his hands—and who now asked him to leave everything.

The familiar market and people of his homeland.

The secure walls and defenses of the City of the Moon.

All his sources of wealth and status.

Doubts. Had there really been a voice in the wind, and was the voice truly Garden-Maker's? Had he understood the message properly? Did Garden-Maker really mean that he must leave the city immediately?

The merchant stood after hearing the strange voice but couldn't move. A cool bath would wash away this afternoon dream. Dream it must have been. Perhaps he secretly wished to flee his life's pressures. Did he wish to escape the disgrace of childlessness? Was he losing his mind?

But beneath question and doubt and rationalization was reality—and the question of courage. Merchant had asked for truth without knowing the price. He looked at his house, his gathered possessions. The value of these versus the value of truth. He grasped a finely glazed earthenware cup, considering its beauty. Then he hurled it against the wall. The sound of its shattering was the voice of his quest, answering fear and self.

He would go.

The sun slipped beyond the horizon when Merchant stepped into his house. He found his wife in the sleeping room and took her soft hands. He rubbed her palms with his thumbs and looked into her beautiful eyes. Did he see there his own reflection?

"I have something to tell you."

He hesitated and swallowed hard.

"I've decided to leave the city and follow truth." There. It was said. And now the words tumbled forth: How he had heard the stories. How he had felt the wind. How he had spoken with Garden-Maker. Would she believe his words?

"I too have sought one who holds the stars in his hands," said Princess. "Now that I know his name I will gladly follow his words."

"Do you wish to go?"

"If the Garden-Maker says to go then we must go."

They said good-bye to family and friends, stowed provisions and valuable possessions into carts. They bought oxen to pull the carts. They purchased sheep and goats and cattle to sustain their future. Then Merchant and his wife, his father and his nephew and their servants left the City of the Moon. The caravan journeyed upriver to the City of Crossroads, stopping by the dwelling of Merchant's older brother. By then they had heard the news that people from the Mountains of the Dawn had ransacked the City of the Moon. The walls were broken and many killed.

At the City of Crossroads they stopped; there Merchant again heard Garden-Maker call.

"Why are you stopping?" asked Garden-Maker.

"My father wishes to visit my older brother," said the merchant.

"Do you walk with your father or do you walk with me?"

"It is the way of my people to show respect to an aged father."

"Respect your father," said Garden-Maker, "but walk with me."

The City of Crossroads was the sister to the City of the Moon. Both were children of the moon and both were ruled by the stars. Merchant's father consulted the priests, who listened to their oracles and advised that he settle among them. He refused to travel another step. Merchant tried to reason with his father, but to no avail. So with a shrug of his shoulders he unpacked the caravan. Years passed and Merchant grew restless for he had not forgotten Garden-Maker's voice. He wanted to follow but his father was old and weak. The merchant cared for him through many illnesses. Then his father died and for seven days the City of Crossroads mourned. The merchant wept but his spirit felt free. Now he could follow Garden-Maker into a new land.

His older brother set his hand on the merchant's shoulder. "Our father has left us great riches," he said. "If you stay in the City of Crossroads, half is yours."

"I must follow the truth and walk with Garden-Maker until he stops."

"The stargazers say Garden-Maker is an empty myth. No one believes in him now."

But Merchant shook his head.

"I have talked with him," he said.

"I have walked with him.

"I have heard his promise."

Merchant looked squarely into his brother's eyes. "If I go I lose my father's inheritance. If I stay, I lose the truth."

Merchant again bid a city good-bye and loaded his possessions into oxcarts and turned his back on wealth. The caravan with Merchant, Princess, his nephew and their servants followed Garden-Maker from the river and across the fertile crescent. Merchant and his caravan walked southwest until Garden-Maker stopped them by a giant oak tree in the grassy hill country north of the City of Palms.

"Sit down in the shade and enjoy the land," said Garden-Maker. "All you see in every direction is yours and your children's. This is where the truth has led you."

"Still I have no children, nor hope of them."

"I am bigger than your hopelessness."

Merchant unpacked his carts and raised his tents. The sheep and cattle grazed. With large stones Merchant built an altar. A spotless newborn lamb was sacrificed as a token of gratitude. As the smoke lifted toward the heavens a gentle rain dampened the grass. The merchant looked up to see a colorful banner stretched above the hills. Ancient stories raced through his thoughts as he remembered Garden-Maker's promise that he is always close and will always care.

BEWARE,
LEST THE SOLUTION
TO THE PROBLEM
BECOME THE PROBLEM.

CHAPTER 3

THE FAMINE

The sun hung hot over the parched hills. Streambeds cracked dry and begged for the briefest of showers, but there was no wisp of cloud in any direction. There had been no rain for two hundred days, and the greens turned brown and shriveled. Without food or water the animals died—at first a few then hundreds then thousands. Finally there were too many to bury in large graves so the corpses bloated in the merciless heat—drawing flies and scavengers, the stench polluting Merchant's new land.

Wells were empty and food scarce. In weeks their reserves would be gone. Half the people were sick, the other half exhausted by heat.

"We must go home," insisted Merchant's nephew, "or at least to the City of Crossroads."

"Garden-Maker led us here," said the merchant.

"Maybe the stargazers are right. Maybe there is no Garden-Maker. We are all going to die. We should have stayed and looked to the moon and stars."

"We have done what is right. Now we must trust; Garden-Maker will not forsake us."

"Most of your herds and flocks are dead. Food and drink are nearly gone. We will all die before the moon completes another cycle."

Merchant walked into his tent and let the door flap drop behind him. Nephew stood outside, fighting the urge to follow. This had to be resolved. But respect and etiquette held him back.

When the land cooled that night, Merchant called all together. "Pack your most necessary possessions," he declared. "When the moon touches the top of the sky we go."

"We go home at last," cheered Nephew.

"No, not home. Garden-Maker led us from the City of the Moon and the City of Crossroads, so we can never go back. We go to the land of the great river delta. They have fertile fields and much water. We will travel at night to reach help before we starve. We must go quickly, so tear down the tents and pack the carts. Leave what you do not need and the herds and flocks—they would not survive the journey."

Merchant began to pack his belongings. He silently folded robes in rough leather bags and muttered to himself.

"I wish we didn't have to travel down to the delta."

"But what is wrong if the land is fertile and there is water?"" asked Princess. "Our family has traded with the merchants of the delta many years."

"Yes, we have, and so I know those people, who desire beautiful women. If a married woman turns their head, they plot against the husband. We will be in danger, for you are very beautiful—your eyes and hair and how you smile."

"You speak as my husband."

"I speak as one who has watched how men watch you."

"Then let us go somewhere else."

"The only other way is to the City of the Moon, and Garden-Maker has closed that door."

"So we starve here or risk the delta?"

"The only safe path is to tell those we meet that you are my sister and not my wife."

Princess became silent. Mechanically she continued to fill bags. Inwardly the force of her husband's words felt as if he had struck her with his fist.

"And if someone wants me?"

"I will be alive to protect you. If I am dead you will be at their mercy."

"So we have no other choice?"

"None," said the man, then added, "but my love for you is deep and strong."

"I know," answered the woman quietly and kissed his cheek.

By night they journeyed south along the ancient trade routes to the great river. In two weeks of dusty travel they reached the beautiful City of the Sun and collapsed at the city's majestic granite gates nearly dead from hunger.

The Delta King pitied the strangers and ordered them revived and brought to the palace. The Delta King was master of his realm and revered by his people as a god. His word was law and disobedience meant death. To live in the rich Land of Deltas meant to follow his rules without hesitation or question.

Merchant knew this as he stood alone in the long and narrow receiving room. His footsteps echoed off golden walls as he slowly made his way through the semidarkness to the massive jeweled throne. Two bronze guards with deadly spears stood on either side of the stone steps which led to the elevated platform and the seat of the Delta King.

"Why have you come?" asked the king in a commanding voice that reverberated off the stone walls.

"We are shepherds from the hill country north of the City of Palms. We seek food and water to escape the great famine."

"Why should the Delta King share the blessings of the divine sun with strangers?"

"We are not strangers. I am the merchant from the City of the Moon. I've traded with you, and my father traded with your father."

"I remember," said the Delta King. "You told the tales of Garden-Maker."

"Now I know more than stories, for I have walked with Garden-Maker."

"So he is real?" The Delta King paused and then said, mostly to himself, "I thought he was a myth from long ago."

"He is real," said Merchant. "He lives beyond the sky and holds the stars in his hands."

"Tonight there will be a festival in the hall of the sun. Come and tell me more of Garden-Maker. And bring your sister, for I hear of her beauty. In the meantime my servants will prepare rooms for your family in the royal palace."

Later that afternoon, Merchant and his family looked west from the palace over flat patchwork pastures and grainfields of green and gold. Beyond the fields flowed the wide rolling river. Farther distant, beyond sight, were the stone monuments that held the bones and belongings of past kings and leaders. The delta people were obsessed with death and each king made certain a royal tomb guaranteed his glorious immortality. The tombs were also monuments to the sun god.

The hall of the sun was simple but elegant. Adjoining the palace, it was spacious with high ceilings and tall archways. Immaculate courtyards and well-tended gardens and crystal-clear pools filled its grounds. Dignitaries in white linen, with collars of colorful beadwork and spangles of silver or gold roved the hall. Servants raced about offering wine from golden goblets. Long, narrow tables were lined with silver platters of exotic foods. Guests ate and drank and mingled to the serenade of seven accomplished harpists.

Many remembered the merchant and his father. They asked Merchant of his travels and why he had left prosperity in the City of the Moon.

"Some things are more important than financial gain," he explained. "We follow the truth and walk with Garden-Maker."

"Who is Garden-Maker?"

"He alone in the universe is infinite and eternal and all-powerful."

"More powerful than the sun?"

"He created the sun."

Trumpets announced the Delta King. The crowd fell silent as the king's procession solemnly paraded into the hall to greet the guests. Dignitaries bowed low and stated their complete, unrestrained loyalty throughout this life and on the eternal journey beyond. At the end of the line stood Merchant and his family. In his turn he stood before the Delta King, saying, "I have asked Garden-Maker to grant you long life and great wisdom."

The room gasped that the god-king would be addressed in such a way. Guards on each side of the royal figure brought their spears to the ready. The king stared at the merchant and the merchant stared back. Then the king looked beyond to Princess. "Who is this woman?" he asked calmly.

"She is my one and only sister, daughter of my father, the merchant from the City of the Moon."

The Delta King kissed her hand gently. "She is a most beautiful woman. I am glad you brought her to the Land of Deltas to share her loveliness with me."

Merchant forced a smile. The room sighed and the guards relaxed.

There was much drinking of wines that night. Gaiety grew spirited and passionate. By the rising of the sun, the Delta King had taken Princess into his royal harem and secured Merchant in his palace room with armed guards outside.

A royal messenger unrolled a small scroll marked with hieroglyphics and cleared his voice. "Because of the merchant's great generosity in the giving of his sister to the Delta King. . ."

"I did not 'give' the princess to the king; he stole her."

". . .I grant him thousands of sheep and thousands of cattle. Plus I grant him grazing rights to the best pasturelands in my realm. . ."

"I don't want any of this. I want Princess returned."

". . .in addition, I grant to Merchant hundreds of donkeys and hundreds of camels and hundreds of the most reliable servants in the great delta."

"I want my sister back!" shouted Merchant. He calmed and struck a reasoned tone. "Tell the king I appreciate his gifts, but I cannot accept them. As soon as he returns my sister, we will be on our way and not bother him any longer."

"If I gave such a reply," said the messenger, "I would die on the spot. And for such an offense the king would publicly execute all your family, including Princess. Accept the god-king's gifts and keep quiet. In a few years he will grow bored. Perhaps you can have her back. The king need not give you anything. He takes what he wants and destroys those who resist. You are greatly favored and can leave the delta with great wealth."

Days turned to weeks and in complete desperation Merchant cried out to Garden-Maker.

"You have waited so long to seek me," said Garden-Maker. "Why did you not ask for relief from the famine or strength for your journey or protection from this land? Your self-sufficiency has caused much suffering."

Merchant bowed his head in shame.

"Now that you have learned, the Delta King must be shown that he is only a man. He can not take whatever he wants."

First it was Delta King's sister who felt the fever's chills. Then her children and her servants. It rapidly worsened to violent nausea and raspy breathing. The royal physicians examined the sick and found swollen glands and poisoned blood.

"It is plague," they told the king in fear. "The sick will certainly die and more will join them quickly. It is the way of this sickness. All you can do is keep the victims away from all who are healthy and hope that it does not spread."

More of the royal family and their servants caught the fever. The king's sister screamed and wailed as the plague infected her brain and drove her mad. Then she slipped into unconsciousness and died. Hours later her servants and children began to die. The king was surrounded by the coughs and cries of the dying, and the palace had become a house of the dead.

The Delta King faced the daybreak sun. "Why? What have we done to offend you?" But the sun did not answer and rose on its daily path as if all was well. Now the king wiped his forehead in horror, for he felt the first fever.

Desperately he ordered anyone who might know what brought the plague to the divine household to step forth. Only one responded—Princess.

Princess looked steadily into his fearful eyes and said, "You, O king, are this source of this sickness. It is sent by Garden-Maker because of your actions against me. You took me into your harem. You touched me, though I am Merchant's wife."

"I did not know. . . ," began the king in horror.

"Had you known, you would have taken me anyway—after killing Merchant. It is as Merchant said it would be, and I see in your eyes that it is true."

The king was silent.

"Garden-Maker takes marriage and commitment seriously. You have offended him."

Merchant was brought to the king immediately.

"You lied to me," said the king, his face red with rage.

"She is my sister, my father's daughter," said the merchant.

"But she is also your wife, and you have brought death to all of my family. Depart my presence and my lands. Take everything I gave you for her. My guards will take you to the end of my realm immediately. But be gone, and perhaps your Garden-Maker will have mercy."

"I will speak with him. But what about my. . ."

"No more talk. Leave me alone and never step into my realm again."

Two large guards threw Merchant violently into the street. The sun glared down and Merchant covered his face. The city bustled past as if he did not exist. Merchant stood and stared at the palace. How could he leave without his wife? But then the doors of the palace opened and Princess was pitched into the street. She groaned as she hit the ground. He reached down to help her, but she pulled away.

So Merchant sat down beside her in the dirt of the street and waited. Minutes passed—hot, dusty, silent minutes; long, uncomfortable, drawn-out minutes. Finally the groans grew into deep, shaking sobs that left her mouth as soft sighs of inner agony. Again she would not accept Merchant's arm.

"You let him take me?" charged the princess with hesitant glances. "You promised to protect me."

The merchant looked at his feet, fumbling with his robe. "I felt I had no choice." He paused and sighed deeply.

"Choices." She glared at him. "What of courage? What of faith in Garden-Maker? Your choice was for safety, never truth."

"What you say is true. I know that now."

"I hated you! I felt too dirty to look at myself. I'm dirty; I'm damaged; I'm ugly."

"You are Princess, as beautiful as the day you became my wife."

"You want me?"

"Will you forgive me? I have offended you and Garden-Maker."

Her face streaked with tears and dirt from the dusty street, the princess leaned toward her husband and dampened his shoulder. He held her tightly.

"Now we return to the land Garden-Maker gave us," said Merchant. "We should not have left. Garden-Maker would have cared for us, even through a terrible famine."

Princess and Merchant walked away from the Delta King's realm, relieved to face home. Behind them trailed a long serpentine caravan, with hundreds of servants and thousands of livestock, creating an ever-growing cloud of dust as they made their way east, with backs aglow from the setting of a bloodred sun.

THE ATTRACTIVE IS OFTEN BESET
WITH HIDDEN COSTS;
CONDITIONS; DANGERS.

‹───◆───›

CHAPTER 4

THE PARTING

The famine was over. Trees lined their limbs with thick layers of white blossoms while a thousand flowers flashed their colors on hillsides and meadows rich with the tender blades of newborn green. Cool, clear water bubbled from natural springs, flowing into pools and down steep streambeds. The merchant had many more sheep and goats in his flocks and cattle and oxen in his herds than before the famine. The journey to the City of the Sun had been morally compromising but financially lucrative. His nephew also had grown wealthy with flocks and herds that were nearly as large as the merchant's.

The family had again pitched their tents near the giant oak. Merchant and Princess and Nephew each sacrificed a spotless newborn lamb on the stone altar and in silence watched the sweet smoke curl its way toward heaven. Garden-Maker looked down and smiled and Shining-One slithered from a deep crevice in a nearby hillside and stared at the three with burning eyes.

All was peaceful.

The trouble began because of their prosperity. Merchant and Nephew had acquired much livestock from the Delta King. Lambs and calves and kids had been born to them. The land could no longer support them. Quarrels erupted over who would graze the green pastures. Quarrels became hostile conflicts.

Cattle were stolen.

Herds were stampeded.

Herdsmen threatened and fought each other.

"What should we do?" asked Nephew. "I've warned my servants but they are so angry. Someone will be hurt."

"We have too many animals. We cannot graze the land as we have, or no grassland will remain."

"We should journey back to the City of Crossroads."

"You know that I will not go back."

"The animals will die."

"This is true," said the merchant. "I think we must divide our livestock and move in different directions."

"We have always been together, since I was a child."

"And I will miss you. But apart we will both prosper. Together our animals will destroy the land and we shall be ruined. You will do well on your own."

Merchant and his nephew stood on the ridge between the hill country and the deep valley of the Winding River, considering what to do next. The hill country was steep and rocky with patches of green. It was fine for sheep, but not good for cattle. The valley had the best grazing for sheep and cattle they had seen since leaving the realm of the Delta King. Thick green grasslands ran right to the edge of the slow-moving winding river as it wound back and forth through the lush countryside before flowing into the Salty Sea. The Winding River was the lowest of all the rivers on the blue planet. An oval plain bounded the Salty Sea. The plain was flat and green with periodic black tar pits where oils would ooze from deep in the earth. On the plain a handful of cities flourished, though they were wicked places that followed the ways of Shining-One.

The two stood on the ridge, silently surveying their options. Finally the merchant spoke. "You make your choice," he said softly. "If you choose east, I'll go west."

Nephew looked at the hill country and then turned toward the fertile valley with its constant supply of water from the wandering river. "I'll take the valley," he said.

"The valley is a good choice, but avoid the cities of the plain. They mock Garden-Maker and walk in darkness. Selfishness has turned their hearts hard."

"I will be careful," said Nephew as he went to gather his possessions.

At first he heeded the words of his uncle. He grazed his livestock near the lush banks of the winding river, but in time he edged south and pitched his tent nearer and nearer to the City of Lime, a prosperous city but the most perverse on the oval plain.

"I'm proud of you," said Garden-Maker to Merchant, "for your self-lessness and generosity to your nephew. Now, look around you. Look north and south and east and west."

The merchant slowly turned to look in every direction. "All I see is land."

"This is the land I give to you and your children and your children's children."

"You speak of inheritance, but who will be my heir?"

"Walk with me and anything is possible. Come, let us walk the length and breadth of the land I've given you," said Garden-Maker. "And as we walk, you'll learn that life is more than what you can see or hear or touch."

So the merchant followed Garden-Maker up and down the narrow footpaths of the new land. They walked every morning as the sun lit the eastern sky, just as Garden-Maker had walked with Man and with Walker so many years before.

They hiked high in the hills thousands of feet above the surface of the oceans. They crossed the ridge and walked down a gentle slope. Here the merchant smelled the sweet scent of honeysuckle and lilacs. Birds sang and a doe with two wobbly fawns drank fearlessly from a still pond. Frogs croaked and jumped from lily pads as the two walkers strolled by.

"This place is beautiful," said Merchant.

"It's called the Valley of Apples, the closest place in likeness to the garden that now exists on the blue planet."

The valley was tucked neatly between two ridges a day's journey south of the City of Palms. With rich soil and many springs, it was a peaceful paradise. Abundant apple and pomegranate and apricot trees blossomed to produce bumper crops. Grapes and melons grew larger than anywhere else in the known world. The place had everything a person would ever want.

"You have been obedient in following the truth. You left the City of the Moon. You left your people when you came to this land. Now you have left your father's household by parting with your nephew. You have done as I asked and so I show you this special place. Because you left so much to walk with me, this will be your new home."

Soon Merchant and Princess and their servants all stood in the Valley of Apples and settled at the lower end near a grove of oaks. With plenty to eat and drink, the animals grew fat and herds and flocks multiplied. Merchant walked with Garden-Maker each morning. And he and the princess were finally at peace.

But there was no peace on the oval plain, where Shining-One ruled.

THE GREATEST HEROISM INVOLVES
SWIFT ACTION AGAINST GREAT ODDS
WITH MORE CONCERN FOR ANOTHER
THAN FOR ONESELF.

CHAPTER 5

THE RESCUE

The world was in turmoil:
Kingdoms rose and fell.
Allies became enemies and then allies again.
Large kingdoms grew fat and small kingdoms grew greedy.

Every unprotected city was a potential target as power-mad kings came to test their mighty armies. They dreamed of war and searched for lands to conquer. Inevitably they saw the cities of the oval plain. A quartet of kings conspired to join and divide as thieves the wealth of this lush prize.

Thousands came from the north on wild, stampeding horses—racing down the valley of the Winding River, slaughtering livestock and capturing everything in their path. Nephew sought safety in the City of Lime, but it was quickly conquered with the rest. Each was required to pay heavy tribute to safeguard their survival. So the towns sent heaps of silver to the kings. But by the thirteenth year, they had forgotten the great invading army. They too could field soldiers, who would throw off their oppressors. They had become strong. So when the messengers came to collect the tribute, they were rebuffed and sent home empty-handed.

The kings immediately sped their armies toward the Salty Sea. The cities of the plain were no match for the mighty kings. They fell fast and hard. The city's leaders fled to the hills as the city was plundered. Everything of value was taken and all that survived within the city gates were enslaved. Among those was Nephew and his family.

One who'd escaped the City of Lime climbed through the western hills to the Valley of Apples. "Your nephew is taken prisoner," the man cried out to Merchant. "The northern kings are taking your nephew back to their land as a slave."

Turning to a nearby servant, the merchant ordered the men under his command to gather. Three hundred well-armed men met outside his tent.

"The armies of the fertile crescent have invaded the oval plain and taken my nephew captive," the merchant's voice shook with anger. "I intend to bring him back. If we move quickly we can cut them off before they turn east at the City of Caravans."

"Against their thousands of soldiers," a husky man shouted. "What chance have a small band of shepherds?"

"We have allies who will stand against this common threat. I've already sent messengers to them. But come or not, ours is the army of Garden-Maker. He alone is our needed ally."

To the sounds of cheers from wives and children, the army of Merchant set out on camels. With steadfast determination they covered over a hundred miles of rocky land. Near the headwaters of the Winding River they caught up with the invaders, who were setting up camp in a long, narrow valley at the foot of a rugged snowcapped mountain. In the twilight, the enemy pitched its tents and lit its fires.

Merchant divided his men and placed them on both sides of the valley. Then they waited for his signal. Darkness surrounded the camp and the invaders clung to their fires, celebrating their conquests with wine and boasts. Almost halfway home and contemptuous of their enemies, they posted few sentries. As their fires died down and the early morning mists grew thick, Merchant ordered his men to mount and attack.

"Oh Garden-Maker," Merchant spoke. "Grant us power and speed."

"I am with you," whispered the wind.

Taking a deep breath he signaled and both groups descended upon the camp from opposite sides. The guards didn't see the charge until a slashing sword made it too late to spread the alarm.

Pandemonium spread through the waking camp. Officers shouted conflicting orders, men stumbled into one another, tents collapsed on their occupants. Camels and horses stampeded everywhere and the furious crash of sword striking sword rang out in the irregular rhythm of battle. In panic the enemy fled up the valley and around the rugged snowcapped eastern mountain. Merchant's men pursued relentlessly with a single mind as far as the large oasis north of the City of Caravans. Here the enemy surrendered.

Merchant freed his nephew and the other citizens of the oval plain. Throwing himself at his uncle's sandaled feet Nephew cried, "Everything I own is yours."

"Get up," said Merchant. "I didn't save you, Garden-Maker did. You owe all to him, for his power won the battle. Without Garden-Maker you would have spent your life in slavery."

Nephew stood and threw his arms around his uncle. "I still want to thank you for coming after me."

The merchant and his men gathered everything the invaders had taken—people, valuables, food, plus the spoils of the army—and headed for home. Between the City of Palms and the City of Lime they were welcomed by all the people, who cheered and danced and shouted as the men came along the road. Flowers littered the road and banners hung from trees. The king of the City of Palms set long tables, overflowing with fresh bread and sparkling wine. Musicians played and people made merry. Merchant and his men were applauded for their bravery.

As day turned to evening, speeches were made. "May Garden-Maker bless Merchant," shouted the king of the City of Palms. "And may you never forget that it was Garden-Maker who delivered the enemy into your hands."

"I will never forget," replied Merchant. "For without Garden-Maker I am dust. Garden-Maker is infinite and eternal and all-powerful. Everything I have was given by him as a token of his absolute ownership; I return to him one-tenth of all I have."

The crowd applauded and the king of the City of Lime spoke. "Because of his great heroism, I grant the merchant all the valuables and food captured from the ruthless invaders."

Again the crowd applauded.

"Thank you for your generosity," replied Merchant. "But I cannot accept your gift. I did not battle the invaders for reward nor to gain favor among those who follow Shining-One. I did it to free my nephew. Besides, Garden-Maker conquered your enemy, not me."

"Look what you're giving up," the king said, pointing to piles of silver and gold.

"Garden-Maker holds more silver and gold in his right hand than you can count in a lifetime. I will be owned by none but Garden-Maker. I will not take from the hands that bow to Shining-One."

"So what is wrong with Shining-One?"

"Shining-One stands against Garden-Maker."

"That's because he says Garden-Maker is cold and cruel and power hungry."

"He is a liar," said the merchant. "You think he makes you happy, but he deceives you."

"You refuse my gift and insult Shining-One," yelled the king, his hand moving to his sword. But he stopped abruptly when the king of the City of Palms quietly stepped between.

"Touch him, and Garden-Maker will destroy you."

"I don't care about Garden-Maker."

"That will be your downfall," said the king of the City of Palms, and turning to Merchant: "Go in peace, beloved of Garden-Maker."

The crowd was silent as the merchant and his men mounted their camels and rode out of the shadowed valley into the western hills where the moon shone bright and the pathway home glittered like the stars.

CHAPTER 6

THE PROMISE

The wind howled through the Valley of Apples and Merchant tossed on his sleeping mat. He stared into the darkness and wrestled with disappointment. Why had his nephew returned to the City of Lime? Didn't he realize that the king and all the people had become twisted as they followed Shining-One? Yet what was most disappointing was the deep sorrow in Princess's eyes.

"I follow Garden-Maker and try to do as he commands. He speaks of future children. But time has run out for my wife and I grieve her empty arms. Will no one carry on my name?"

A glow illuminated the tent. Merchant sat up and heard a soft, clear voice whisper his name. He grabbed the sword beside his bed and leaped to his feet. Princess did not stir in her tent, and no alarm was heard. He burst outside.

"You need no weapons here," came a familiar and beloved voice from the darkness. Merchant tossed his sword to the side and walked out into the night.

"Why have you come, Garden-Maker?"

"I am always here. But tonight I wish to calm your heart and confirm my promises."

"A calm heart is not always easy to maintain."

"I will be your comfort and your shield," said Garden-Maker. "I can give you rewards greater than the riches offered by any king. You wisely rejected the king of the City of Lime. This king could never imagine the rewards I give to those who follow me. He covets only Shining-One."

"The only reward I desire is a son and grandchildren. I have adopted a son from the City of Caravans. He is a good man and is in charge of everything I own. He will inherit all and carry on my heritage."

"This man will not be the son I promised. When the time is right you shall hold your own child.

"Trust me.

"Follow me.

"Let me shape the future

"—or more tears will dampen your path."

Garden-Maker and Merchant faced each other under the glittering sky, the infinite and the finite. "Look up from the blue planet and tell me what you see."

"Stars. Many, many stars."

"How many?"

"As a stargazer I counted thousands."

"If your eyes had been pure, you could have seen thousands more. So numerous will I make the descendants of your seed. I have promised a son and a land for your descendants. You will have both."

"It just seems impossible. My wife has empty arms. And others claim the land."

"Impossibilities have never stopped me from keeping my word. Do you question my ability? My sincerity?"

"I only wonder. . .why. . .you do these things for me."

"Because I love you."

The two walked and talked through the heat of the day and as the last light of the sun disappeared they agreed: Merchant would walk with Garden-Maker, while Garden-Maker would give Merchant a son and a land.

Ten summers passed.

Princess's long black hair thinned and grayed. Its shimmer faded.

She was far beyond childbearing. All of Merchant's consoling whispers to be patient could not change that irreversible fact.

For ten torturous years—more than three thousand days—she waited. Her limit was reached.

"Husband, divorce me. You must."

"I will not break my commitment to you," said Merchant in exasperation.

"I have failed in my commitment to bear your heir. Garden-Maker promised a son from your seed. That son will not emerge from my body. It must come from another. Garden-Maker only spoke of your seed, not my womb."

"He knows you are my wife."

The woman knelt before her husband and held his gaze as she said what she had reasoned through so carefully.

"We have adopted a son, but he does not fulfill Garden-Maker's words. We have tried these many years to use my body. That choice is no longer real. One way remains. Accept my youthful handmaiden as your son's mother."

"It is not right. I hurt you when I spoke of choices in Egypt. I won't do anything that will hurt you anymore."

Yet Princess still refused to give up. She pressed at every opportunity until Merchant was tired and confused and frustrated. So one night he reluctantly held out his hand to his wife's servant. She accepted it, and they walked off together.

Princess had won but she felt no victory. Tension built with her mate. And did she not notice a new glint in the handmaiden's eye, a lilt in her step, a confidence in her voice? Princess tried to ignore it, but she couldn't. She watched the handmaiden braid her thick black hair, place beige coloring on her flawless complexion and giggle with the other servants.

Youth.

Beauty.

And yes, the first signs of a baby inside.

Why had the Delta King given her this highbred girl during their stay in the City of the Sun? It seemed his final curse on her life.

Princess might have borne her thoughts in silence, but her husband took delight in the progress of his child. He closely observed the growth of the handmaiden's stomach. He felt the bulging contour of her abdomen, amazed at the miracle of life. His voice was gentle, almost intimate, when he asked how she felt. His eyes brightened when she entered the room. No longer a faceless handmaiden, she was the lovely mother of his only child. He watched her do her daily tasks and suggested that Princess lighten her work. The whole valley treated the handmaiden with special respect.

Merchant was congratulated.

The handmaiden doted upon.

The princess forgotten.

All this infuriated Princess. The expectant mother moved too slowly, smiled insolently, and acted independently. She was gloating, for she had done in a moment what Princess could not in a lifetime. Her servant laughed at her. She was sure of it. "I can't take this any longer. She mocks. She ridicules me."

Merchant knew his wife too well to question her words. "We will work things out," he comforted. "I love you and want no shadow between us. She could live in the upper valley. We have a responsibility to the child, but he doesn't have to be raised as our son."

"But what about an heir?"

"Garden-Maker has promised an heir and he will provide one."

The next morning the handmaiden sat on a rock with her bare feet dangling in the still cool water of a public spring. Female servants gathered about, laughing and stroking the firm rounded stomach.

"Did you feel that?" asked the handmaiden.

"Yes, he just kicked," said a servant. "And there, again."

Princess's face burned and she pushed through the knot of servants, who scattered quickly and silently. She grabbed the expectant mother by both shoulders and shook her, "It's my baby, not yours. Don't ever forget that."

The girl returned her glare coolly. "But it was planted in my body."

"As soon as you deliver, it will belong to me. And if you continue to mock me, you will never see my child again."

"I won't let you do that."

Princess slapped her hard across the face.

The handmaiden rushed away from the spring. Tears streaming down her cheeks she walked blindly, as fast as her condition would allow. Oh to return to the Land of Deltas. Yes, she must go home. Drying her tears, she repeated her resolution and turned south. She forced herself forward under an unforgiving sun as the sand scorched her unprotected feet. Her lower back ached with each dusty step. The heat lodged in her throat, burning away her saliva and cracking her tender lips. In the distance she saw swaying palm trees. If she could reach that oasis, there would be water. It not, she and her child would die.

Her legs collapsed. She clutched her stomach with her last ounce of energy as she hit the ground. Then all faded. Perhaps this was death, for she felt coolness and relief. Sweet liquid moistened her mouth. Energy stirred in her exhausted body and her eyes slowly opened. Before her stood something that she could only think was an angel of the ancient stories—twice as tall as a man with a glowing aura that shone about him. He had strong, masculine features and calm, gentle eyes. His golden hair danced in the breeze.

The handmaiden sat up and stared in awe at her strange savior. Questions crowded, but it seemed irreverent to speak. So she sat in silence as he ministered to her. Minutes passed, maybe hours, before a soft, ethereal voice drifted to her mind:

"Handmaiden, where do you belong?"

"I'm running from the princess, sir." The servant detected no hatred toward a runaway slave in this person, but she could not have lied. "My mistress is jealous and treats me harshly. I carry the merchant's son and she is jealous."

"So, Handmaiden, where do you belong?"

"I want to go back to the land of my parents."

"But where do you belong?"

"I belong with the princess, I am her handmaiden."

"Return to where you belong, and my master will bless you."

She was alone. The handmaiden rubbed her eyes and stood, refreshed. As the sun fell to the west she journeyed back to the Valley of Apples, to the place she belonged. Soon she gave birth to a boy. She held him close to her breast and kept him quiet. Her head was bent and her voice only spoke in whispers. She didn't want to draw Princess's attention. Her life was her child and he was all she needed.

But the child was not taken from her, and thirteen summers passed, in which Merchant watched his son grow tall and strong. He loved this son and was perplexed at why Garden-Maker refused to see in this boy the fulfillment of his promise.

"Walk with me," came the voice as the sun touched the roof of the sky.

"It is the hottest time of the day," said Merchant. But he set down his work.

"You have known me as Garden-Maker," said the voice as they climbed the hills, "but I have other names. To you I will be Promise-Keeper. We have agreed: You will walk with me; I will give a son and a land to you."

"You have given me a son."

"You tried to give me a son. I will give you a son through the wife of your youth."

"The spring of our youth has been forgotten in the depths of winter. My princess has had empty arms all her days. She is long past the age of giving birth."

"So you think it is impossible?" asked the Promise-Keeper. "Recall my words of years ago: 'Impossibilities have never stopped me from keeping my word.'"

"I have waited through each of those years."

"Yes, though not always patiently. There is a perfect time and when that time comes I will act. I have promised you many descendants, and I am Promise-Keeper. From this day you will no longer be Merchant. I rename you Father and your wife Mother. For the two of you will parent a powerful nation with descendants as vast as the starry sky."

The old man's head was bent and his heart yielded.

"Years ago we agreed in this very valley. I declare that this agreement is between me and all your descendants. Yet people forget and break promises. So there will be a sign of commitment that can be seen and not forgotten."

"What kind of sign?"

"A symbol will be cut into flesh to remind you and your descendants of your eternal commitment with Promise-Keeper. Cut each male's body at the source of the next generation—the seed.

"Let the pain be a token of the pain I feel when my people do not walk with me.

"Let the blood be a token of what the deer shed so long ago in the garden.

"Let there be a life-lasting mark as a token that they belong to me forever.

"You and your wife will bear a son and his descendants will carry out the cut of commitment, so that our agreement will never be forgotten. It will be a mark that they wear for eternity."

The two returned to the place where they began, and the voice of Promise-Keeper vanished with the wind. Merchant, now Father, went out that day and marked himself with the cut of commitment. He marked Handmaiden's Son and all his male servants.

cappprox

CHAPTER 7

THE CITY

Merchant liked his new name of Father. It gave him hope, though his hope sounded ridiculous. He pondered the words of Promise-Keeper and wondered how to share them with his wife. If he told her the new names Promise-Keeper had given them, she would laugh the laughter of bitterness.

He leaned back in the shade of his tent, watching through the blur of heat waves the browns and yellows of the dusty road into the valley. He sipped fresh springwater from a clay cup and stroked his gray beard as he stared into the distance. Someone was coming, but it must be a mirage, for no one traveled during the hottest time of the day except in dire need. Father rubbed his eyes and strained his vision. Two men. . . no, three. . . walked his way. Actually they appeared to float several feet above the road, treading on the shimmery ground heat.

Strangers rarely came through the Valley of Apples and when they did the event required all affordable hospitality. Father jumped to his feet and walked briskly to meet the three men. "It's much too hot to walk these hills when the sun is so high," he said to the three.

"We have traveled far," said the leader.

"Come and rest in the shade of my oaks," said Father. "My servants will bring cool water to quench your thirst and soak your feet."

The three followed Father to his tent. Water was brought and food prepared. Servants baked fresh bread and slaughtered a calf. Fruit and cheeses were laid out on a silver tray. After a wonderful meal the leader asked, "Where is your wife—she who is Mother?"

"You know her new name?"

"I know all things," said the leader. "And I remind you that you and your wife will have a newborn son by this time next year."

Princess, who was eavesdropping from behind the door to the tent, laughed. She quickly pulled back to the shadows, hoping no one had heard, and covered her mouth to muffle her reaction.

"Why does your wife laugh?"

"We are old and my wife is beyond childbearing years."

"Promise-Keeper swore to you."

"How do you know. . . ? I have not repeated his words even to my wife."

"Bring her to me and I will tell her." Father brought out his wife and the leader of the three repeated all the words of Promise-Keeper.

Mother stood in silent disbelief. "Thirty summers ago this news would have thrilled my heart, now—impossible! No, it's too late for me." Her words were unspoken, but the man seemed to hear them.

"Impossibilities have never stopped Promise-Keeper from keeping his word."

Those were the words of Promise-Keeper, thought Father. He did not hesitate but fell on his face before the men in fear. He had spoken with Promise-Keeper before, but now that presence was unhid. He did not belong near this visitor. He would be unmade. Mother did not have as much knowledge of the words, but she understood her husband's reaction and dropped to her knees.

"Fear does not belong with friendship," the man said with a sedate smile, "and we are all friends here."

As the four walked into the hills the two remained silent and seemed to shimmer as if struggling to hold substance.

"Beyond the sky and beyond time all creatures are spiritual," explained Promise-Keeper, pointing to his companions. "Angels have no shape or substance, so they can take any form. We came to test your spirit and see what kindness you would offer strangers. Your heart has been generous and your spirit kind," the words of Promise-Keeper took a more quiet and serious tone:

"Now my angels go to test other hearts and spirits in the city."

The two immediately broke away. They strolled purposefully toward the road that led down the hill and toward the oval plain.

A vague unease gnawed at Father.

"To what city do they travel?" he asked. He and Promise-Keeper had reached a vantage high in the hills, where the plain stretched before them and the Salty Sea was a distant emerald.

"That city." Promise-Keeper pointed in the direction of the distant City of Lime.

"The blue planet has many cities. Why do they test that one?"

"That city is great in the ways of Shining-One. Its people mock me and walk in violence and anarchy. For such wickedness I once washed evil from the blue planet. Selfishness has turned their hearts to stone."

"All that is true of many cities," said Father.

"The City of Lime has the hardest of hearts. With each year, their rebellion and callousness grow."

"And if the people fail the test?"

"They will be swept away. No longer will they spread poison to other valleys of the blue planet, where some still value truth above self-indulgence. If they fail the test, the cities of the plain will show that my ways cannot be trampled forever."

"But what if there are people with sensitive hearts who refuse the ways of Shining-One? Will you consume fifty pure hearts with the wicked city?"

"I will spare the plain and its people for fifty who follow."

"What if there are forty-five who long to walk with you, but simply don't know how?"

"I will spare it for forty-five who desire."

"Perhaps forty have fallen and been deceived by Shining-One. But they see their error and plead your forgiveness."

"I will spare it for forty who plead forgiveness."

"What if there are only twenty?"

"If there are even ten, I will spare all."

"Your compassion is immense," said Father.

"I would rejoice if the City of Lime holds ten pure hearts that would walk with me in the morning and follow my footpaths through the highlands."

As twilight turned the oval plain gray, Promise-Keeper disappeared. All that was left of his presence was a gentle breeze and a sweet aroma. Father lingered on the ridge watching the plain in the growing darkness and wondering about his nephew. He had lived there twenty-five summers and was a city elder. His wife seemed wonderful and his daughters beautiful. But they all had known the pull of compromise in the midst of evil. Were their hearts pure? He walked toward home to face the fretful questions of a woman who had laughed at Promise-Keeper—and who desperately longed to be called "Mother."

And two travelers arrived at a city gate where Nephew took his turn keeping watch.

"Who is there?" asked Nephew.

"Two strangers, tired after a long day's journey," came the response.

"I will shelter you at my house, the city has nowhere else to rest at this hour. We have cool water to quench your thirst and soak your feet. My wife will serve you a hearty meal. After a good night's sleep you can be on your way."

"We will not trouble you," said the two. "We will just rest in the town square."

"That," said Nephew. "would not be safe. The City of Lime is known for its violence toward strangers. They are robbed and beaten and worse, and no one here will intervene. This is a people without concern and without conscience. Stay with my family."

The visitors followed him to their host's house and ate a late dinner. Nephew and his wife visited with these curious travelers until a rock suddenly crashed against the shutters that covered the window opening.

"Stay down," cautioned Nephew, grave concern reflected on his face.

"What is wrong?" asked one of the visitors.

"Someone has seen you come, and now they want you."

"If they want to see us, we will go out to them."

"You don't understand," said the wife. "There are men, many of them —who prowl the night looking for anyone—woman or man—on whom to satisfy their lusts. They have seen two young men, tall and handsome, and that could drive them wild."

The view from the gap between the shutters was wild and frightening. A large crowd of men, some young and some old, pelted the house of mud and plaster, shouting demands. Their torch-lit shadows turned the night red with the appearance of blood and anarchy. They cursed and waved fire. Others stood back in the shadows, until the narrow street fronting the house overflowed with inflamed rioters.

Fists pounded doors and shutters. These feeble protections would soon give way.

"What do you want?" cried out Nephew.

"The strangers," yelled back one who with a twisted leer, who seemed to lead the crowd. "Bring them out and the rest of you can live."

"You would kill us all?"

"Hurry or we'll burn your house and trample its ashes." Others jeered and made lewd, drunken gestures and whipped their torches excitedly. They were in danger of setting all the city ablaze.

"Let me come out to talk."

"Then we'll warm up on you," laughed the man with the snaky grin.

Nephew took up a club and a knife and slowly slipped through the door to face the threatening mob.

"No talk," yelled one of the men. "We know what we want so give it now."

"Don't some of you have parents or wives that you shame? These strangers have come under my protection. I cannot allow their harm."

"You can't stop us," someone shouted back. The crowd howled and cackled in chaotic abasement. "Who are you to judge us? You are an outsider. You speak of Garden-Maker and what is right. So you do what you think is right—and we'll do what we think is right."

The serpentine grin yelled, "Let's do it," and the crowd surged forward. But suddenly they stopped in overwhelming awe. For alongside Nephew stood two pillars of light, as bright as the sun.

Gasps burst from the startled swarm, and the log that was to be their battering ram dropped. Tormented eyes searched for the comfort of darkness. Streams of dazzling white-hot light overpowered the feeble flaming torches. Radiating arcs of phosphorescent arrows forced the mob back with burning flares that singed their faces, scorching cheeks to an unnatural ruddy hue. Men covered their eyes and turned their backs. Those foolish enough to look screamed in pain and panic as the brilliant intensity burned away their vision. Men trampled one another in their chaotic flight of fear and confusion.

The angelic glory faded and the two took the speechless nephew back into the dwelling.

"We are sent by Garden-Maker to determine the fate of this city. We see four hearts tainted but willing to be pure. Are there others?"

"My daughters are engaged to good young men."

"Are there more?"

"I know of none."

"Go to these men quickly and tell them to flee the city and the valley. The time to purify has come."

Nephew ran to rouse the men pledged to his daughters and to beg them to flee the city. "Garden-Maker is about to sweep it all away."

Both young men laughed. "More Garden-Maker nonsense? You've had too much wine, old man. It's the middle of the night. Go home and sleep it off."

"But two angels are at my house! They say. . ."

"Angels? What a fool," each said in turn. "Leave us alone and we'll talk tomorrow."

"We won't be here tomorrow," insisted Nephew. "You must come now."

At both dwellings the young men laughed and slammed the door in Nephew's face.

The old man ran home with tears in his eyes. He loved these men as sons. Why wouldn't they listen?

The sun glowed bloody red on the eastern horizon, then was shrouded in black, billowy storm clouds. Lightning slashed the distant sky and an eerie calm settled over the city as if warning of its approaching fate.

"Hurry!" shouted one of the angels. "The storm is coming. Grab your wife and daughters. You have no more time."

Nephew looked at the luxuries of his ease in this place.

What to save and what to leave?

What did he need? What did he want?

What would he miss the most?

So many things—everyday items and valuables, memories and rolls of writings, tools and clothes and food. Nephew's wife gathered together a pile of belongings and his girls wandered the house, picking up their favorite treasures. Then the earth shook with such violence that Nephew was thrown into the wall.

"Drop what you hold and run," warned an angel. "It's beginning."
The angels grabbed the hands of the family and compelled them through

the front door—just before the roof collapsed.

The City of Lime was built on a crack deep in the earth. It ran beneath the Winding River, the Salty Sea and south to the great ocean beyond. Earth forces had heaved against their confinement for millennia, awaiting this one moment of release. Crevices opened and swallowed houses whole. The earth buckled and buildings tumbled and trees sank. Those who survived the first shaking crushed one another in their flight as the earth rose and fell like the ocean in a gale.

Through the devastation the angels led Nephew and his family out the city gates to the surrounding countryside. Close behind, hidden in the dust, slithered the serpent, escaping the city that was crumbling because of his deceptions. He had been master here and was sorry to go, but the tricks he had learned there would help him rule in other hearts.

"Only in the highlands will you be safe," the angels implored. "Run and don't turn back, not even for a moment."

Out of the eastern sky a long jagged bolt of lightning struck the ground not far behind them. The ground exploded, sending red-hot chunks of salt sailing through the early morning air. Nephew and his family ran faster. Again lightning struck the ground behind them, this time setting off a greater explosion. Each lightning flash ignited the mixture of sulfur and salt, tar and oil, propelling molten projectiles into buildings with deafening impact that shook the ground like aftershocks. The sky blazed with a dirty orange hue as the entire town was engulfed in smoke and flames.

Nephew felt the heat at his back and kept his face toward the highlands in fear as he remembered the angel's words, "Don't look back." Other thoughts raced through the mind of his wife, with her breath ragged from running and her face streaked with tears. Lost were her home and her belongings and her friends. She had heard the angel's warning, but she slowed for just a few heartbeats to catch her breath and during that moment she glanced toward the city. At that instant lightning flashed and the earth around her exploded. Her scream was drowned by the blast that caught her at its center. She died instantly as burning sulfur and salt melted her skin and entombed her. Days later Nephew and his daughters found her remains enshrined on the plain in a memorial of hardened salt.

Far above and miles distant, Father and Promise-Keeper walked the western ridge and looked down on the oval plain. Thick clouds of smoke rose, and distant rumbling explosions could be heard. Father hung his head. "There were not even ten?"

"I wish there were," said Promise-Keeper. "I truly wish there were."

TRUST LETS GO AND
ALLOWS SOMEONE ELSE
TO MAKE THE DECISIONS
THAT CONTROL OUR FUTURE.

CHAPTER 8

THE SON

The beautiful Valley of Apples was the home of Father and Mother for years upon years. They had known its few people, feasted on its fruit and increased their herds and flocks. But the time had come to move. Once more the faithful couple packed their belongings into simple ox-drawn carts and headed up the valley, over the western mountains and down the other side. Wide, flat coastal plains spread before them and beyond lie the twinkling blue of the Great Sea. In this land lived the sea people, aggressive and mean-spirited followers of Shining-One. Father and Mother settled on the eastern edge of the plain, a few days' journey southwest of the Valley of Apples. Here there was more room for their herds and flocks to graze. Father pitched his tents near a wet-weather stream and thanked Promise-Keeper for safe journeys and a new home.

Mother came behind him and rubbed his tired shoulders. "I like my new name," she spoke softly.

"The name and the promise," added Father as he took her hand.

"I should not have laughed at his words."

"At times we doubt Promise-Keeper, but in the end his words always come true."

"And they have," said Mother. "A child now grows inside my body."

With a gasp of joy Father lifted her off the ground and swung her around. He kissed her and held her close as his heart beat a hundred times faster than normal.

"It is as Promise-Keeper said, 'Impossibilities have never stopped me from keeping my word,'" he whispered, holding her in his arms and suddenly feeling the miracle of the moment. That evening bonfires flamed high as the camp celebrated with food and wine and dancing until the sun began its fiery journey across the heavens.

When the time was right and the baby was ready, a ninety-year-old woman gave birth to a flailing boy with strong lungs. A one-hundred-year-old father looked on in utter amazement. What a miracle of life had graced the two most-unlikely of parents. Princess had laughed because it was impossible. Now she laughed because the impossible was true. She named her son Laughter.

With trembling hands and rainwashed eyes the man held his promised son. Staring into the tiny face, he smiled and pressed lips to the infant's soft forehead. Eight dawns later Father sharpened the gleaming silver of his best blade. Then with tenderness and precision he gave his newborn child the cut of commitment.

Mother loved and nurtured and protected her baby as he grew his first inches and cut his first teeth and threw his first tantrums. When it was time to leave his mother's warmth and be weaned, Father threw a dinner party and invited all from miles around. It was a joyous occasion and gifts were lavished on the child of promise. Father greeted his guests with warm embraces and Mother showed off her son. But the child was shy and quiet and hid behind his mother's long robe. He resisted her efforts to coax him out and kept to the shadows. On the edge of the crowd she saw that Handmaiden's Son, strong and handsome, was the center of attention among the young women. For fifteen years the handmaiden had cared for her son quietly. Now he was growing up and had his own mind. Women competed for his attention as he spoke with confidence and held his head high.

Mother looked at her withdrawn toddler then at the proud son of her handmaiden. Years of buried anger surfaced as her face burned red with rage. She grabbed her son's small hand and pulled him into her tent. After the guests slept, Mother confronted her husband.

"I can't stand that woman or her frivolous son. Send them away. I just want them gone."

"The handmaiden's boy is also my son."

"You have only one real son and one genuine heir. No insolent half-breed will share Laughter's inheritance."

"Go to sleep and early in the morning, when I walk with Promise-Keeper, I will ask what to do."

"I live beyond the sky," echoed Promise-Keeper as the sun stretched over the eastern hills. "I hold the stars in my hands. Certainly I am able to care for both your sons."

"But my wife wants me to send away the handmaiden and her boy."

"Do as she asks."

"They will be killed by wild animals or captured by bandits or die of exposure and starvation."

"Not if I nurture and strengthen them as I say I will. Laughter will inherit this land and his descendants will be known as my people. Yet Handmaiden's Son also will flourish. He will rule the surrounding lands and his descendants will be as plentiful as the sands of the desert."

Father packed cakes and fruit and cheese into a leather bag. He filled large skins with water. To the handmaiden, he spoke gently. "The time has come for change. You and your son must leave the camp."

"Our son," she corrected without malice.

"Our son."

"We have done no wrong. But I will do what you wish. I only want a good home for our son."

Father set his wrinkled hand on the boy's shoulder and embraced his son, saying, "Follow your mother. Promise-Keeper has said he will watch over you and guide you to greatness."

The handmaiden and her son walked south toward the Land of Deltas. The day was hot and the next was hotter. The way was rough and everything looked the same. They wandered in circles through the dusty desert until their water ran out. Their feet hurt and their tongues swelled. Their minds played tricks on them as they saw pools of refreshing water surrounded by palm trees. They ran to the edge of the mirage and waded into the disappointment of illusion. Both collapsed into the suffocating heat and the boy fell into delirium.

With trembling arms the handmaiden carried her child to the shade of a small tamarisk tree. She pushed back his hair and wiped his forehead. He muttered something slurred and she kissed his cheek. Then she walked away with tears in her eyes, far enough that she couldn't hear his ragged breathing and confused cries. There was nothing she could do to save her son. So she sat dispirited in the harsh midday sun and sobbed.

A black and white vulture waited in the upper branches of the tamarisk tree.

A scorpion skittered by.

A serpent watched with keen eyes and an arrogant smile.

But the handmaiden saw none of these things. Nor did she focus on the large man who stood over her with golden hair and large shimmering robe and a brightly glowing face. "Handmaiden," his voice resonated, "what is wrong?"

"My son dies," she rasped as if to herself.

"Promise-Keeper has heard your son's cries. He won't let the boy die. Lift your head and look over to that hill."

The handmaiden shook her head. "There is nothing but another mirage."

"The water of Promise-Keeper is always real."

The angel walked to the unconscious boy and effortlessly picked him up and strolled toward the waters. The woman slowly stumbled behind, wanting to believe but afraid she was living a fevered dream. But when she dipped her feet into the cool water she screamed in delight. She splashed the water in her face and drank deeply. Then she raised her son's head and trickled water past the boy's cracked lips and into his mouth. He groaned and sipped the liquid greedily.

When they were fully conscious the angel was gone. They sat by the spring and thanked Promise-Keeper for his provision. The next morning they continued their journey, reaching the trade route to the City of the Sun. In time Handmaiden's Son became a mighty man, and his twelve sons became powerful kings over the great desert of the east.

The next years passed quickly and were filled with joy in the family of Father and Mother and Laughter. Mother had rocked her son to sleep and Father had guided his first stumbling steps. Now he was thirteen summers old, with his own thoughts and dreams. Every morning as the sun spread golden on the hilltops, Father and son walked with Promise-Keeper. The three shared their hearts without embarrassment or misunderstanding or rejection.

One evening as Father relaxed, he felt a cool breeze off the Great Sea and heard the old familiar voice of Promise-Keeper call his name.

"Here I am."

"Tomorrow you must take a walk for me, your hardest journey."

"Where will you lead me?"

"North to a rocky hilltop in the high country near the City of Palms. On that hilltop I will ask you to sacrifice what you love most."

"Shall I bring a spotless newborn lamb?"

"No," said Promise-Keeper. "This sacrifice will be more precious than a lamb."

"All my sheep?

"All my cattle?

"All my oxen?"

"No," said Promise-Keeper. "This sacrifice will be more precious than all your animals."

"Whatever is mine you can take."

"I will take your son."

Father's heart paused and he felt terribly sick and he dropped to his knees in weakness.

"Oh please, is there some other way?" he asked hopefully.

"Tomorrow morning get up earlier than normal and chop enough wood to burn a sacrifice; take your son and follow me. On the altar of sacrifice you will offer your son to the one who is above all things."

"This is the son of promise. He is your miracle and blessing and the future of your people. Please don't ask this," begged Father. "Let me die in his place. I'm old and have lived a good life. My son is a child. If he dies, I will die."

"Will you follow me?"

"I can't hurt my son."

"Will you follow me?"

"I want to, but how can you. . ."

"Will you follow me?"

"Yes," said Father in angry resignation.

"Then trust me."

Father could not sleep that night. He slipped into his son's tent and stood above his bed and watched his boy's peaceful slumber. Why would Promise-Keeper have him sacrifice the very child who was to provide descendants as plentiful as the stars? This made no sense. Unless. . .unless he would bring the boy back from death. But that was impossible. Except impossibilities did not keep Promise-Keeper from doing what he said.

Promise-Keeper's words, "Trust me," washed across his mind. He either trusted Promise-Keeper or he didn't. There was no halfway commitment with the one who lived beyond the sky. Behind was a lifetime of promises kept and impossibilities overcome and hope affirmed.

Ahead was anxiety. Sometime during the night Father handed all he had, even his son, into the care of the one who cares. Somehow all would work out. His fears faded and a peaceful sleep soothed his spirit.

Arising early, Father split wood for the sacrifice. With son and servants he followed Promise-Keeper north to the highlands. For three days they walked until they saw the hill of sacrifice.

"My son and I must now walk alone," said Father to the servants. "Remain until we return at sunset."

Confidence and fear.

Trust and horror.

Waiting and wondering.

Father and son climbed the steep hillside. Son struggled under the burden of firewood but said nothing. As the two saw the outcropping of rock at the top, Laughter asked, "Where is our sacrifice?"

"Promise-Keeper will provide."

Father aimed his eyes forward and focused his heart on two small words: "Trust me."

Now on the hilltop of sacrifice the two looked at each other in silence. The son felt his father's waves of sorrow as the two carefully and wordlessly and slowly fit large stones to build a simple altar. Only the wind was heard as they stacked the wood on the stones.

"What do we do now?" asked the boy.

"We obey Promise-Keeper," said Father.

"What does he have us do?"

"I am to sacrifice you on this altar."

The son stared at his father and then at the altar. His face paled and his chin quivered. Then he tightened his jaw and faced his father.

"Promise-Keeper is infinite and eternal and all-powerful. What he says is truth and what he asks is right."

"From you must come descendants as plentiful as the stars," replied

Father slowly. "So I know that what I do will be undone. If you die and your flesh rises with the flames Promise-Keeper will remake your body and breathe new life back into you. He must or he is Promise-Breaker."

"What must I do?"

"Forgive me for what I'm about to do."

Son embraced his father and they clung together.

"You have the greater burden," Laughter said. "You may use the knife and then stand on this mountain alone. You will be left to face the wind and walk away." The boy extended his arms to be tied. "My task is fearful, but I could not do yours."

Father lifted his son's strong body and set him upon the altar.

"It would be easier if you close your eyes," said Father.

Laughter squeezed his eyes shut as his father pulled his knife, its heavy bronze blade honed sharp, from its sheath of leather at his side.

He stood before his son.

He clutched the handle of his knife with both hands.

He aimed its point at the boy's heart for a swift and painless death.

Then he raised his arms toward the sky. "Promise-Keeper, I follow you," he whispered, then gritted his teeth and quickly sliced downward with a heart-wrenching groan. Suddenly his arms were restrained in midair, as by a hidden hand.

"Stop!" The voice of Promise-Keeper thundered across the mountain. Father released a strong sigh.

"Lay down your knife! And don't let it touch the boy."

The knife clattered to the ground.

"You followed me, though it meant sacrificing what you loved most."

Suddenly Father heard snorting and bleating and branches breaking behind him. He turned to confront a wild ram caught by his horns in a thicket not more than twenty paces away. The animal shook his head frantically and pushed his hoofs hard against the rocks, trying to back out of the underbrush. The harder the ram struggled, the tighter the thicket held.

"Here is your sacrifice," said Promise-Keeper. "Release your son and take him back from death."

Father cut the ropes and lifted his boy from the altar. He freed the ram and sacrificed it to Promise-Keeper. The smoke drifted high above the land and the wind spoke:

"Father, you have walked the hardest road and you have not strayed nor stumbled. To you who follow me without holding back I give descendants as plentiful as the stars that sparkle through the dark. Through your descendants I give hope to the hopeless of the blue planet."

Father smiled at his son.

"Let's go home."

The two held hands and walked down the trail as the setting sun cast stretched-out shadows across the smoldering stones atop the hill of sacrifice.

AMAZING CIRCUMSTANCES
ARE ORCHESTRATION RATHER THAN ACCIDENT—
FOR UNSEEN FORCES WORK ONE STEP AHEAD,
PREPARING EVERY PATH.

CHAPTER 9

THE BRIDE

Father, let's go home."

"This is home. We've lived here thirty-five summers."

"The Valley of Apples is home."

"But we have too many flocks and herds to move back to the valley."

"Sell them or hire someone to manage them," said Mother. "But I must go home, for my days are short and I will soon leave the blue planet."

Within a month the couple pulled their oxen-drawn carts back into the Valley of Apples. The blossoming trees and wildflowers remained lovely. Father and Mother sat in the shade of oaks remembering joys and sorrow. True to his word, Promise-Keeper had given them a son. Their son was now a quiet man, gentle and reserved. He still walked mornings with his father and Promise-Keeper. At other times he withdrew into himself.

"He looks so lonely," Mother told her husband. "He needs a companion to walk beside him and make him laugh."

"I walk beside him," said Father.

"He needs a bride. You have made me happy in our togetherness. He should enjoy a kindhearted wife to give him love and warmth and children."

"But most women within several days' journey follow the ways of Shining-One. They say there is no Garden-Maker. Many have not even heard his new name."

"But to give descendants, he needs a wife."

"He will have a wife," said Father. "But she must be a special woman who is willing to follow the truth wherever it may take her."

"Please . . ." Mother hesitated. Her eyes seemed to focus on something far away and her body began to lose its balance.

Father quickly put his arms around her and gazed into her eyes.

Her voice was weak. "Please. . ." she started again, slowly marking each word—"find. . .our son. . .a. . ."

A quiet cough tickled her throat and her eyes grew cloudy. She blinked herself to a last moment of clarity and whispered, ". . .a. . . bride."

"I will," said Father as he kissed her wrinkled hand. "He will be blessed by Promise-Keeper indeed if he finds a woman half as wonderful as you."

Mother smiled and her eyes fluttered a final farewell. She relaxed into his arms, slipping silently from her well-worn body.

That day Father bought one of the best parcels of land in the valley for a large bag of silver. It was an extreme price because the seller assumed the buyer would bargain him down. But Father was too grieved to follow custom. The land had a field and trees, a large cave and a peaceful view. Father carried his wife up the western slope of the valley, through the wide circular opening and into the dark cool shadows of the cave. Gently he laid her delicate body in the cave and wept. Roses and daylilies were scattered over her form until she disappeared beneath the fragrant petals. Father sealed the opening and sat outside for hours and wondered why life was so hard.

"Long ago in the garden life was not so hard," said Promise-Keeper. "Then a choice was made, bringing pain and sorrow to the blue planet."

"Sometimes it is too heavy to bear."

"Walk with me and I will share your weight."

Father walked and Promise-Keeper shared his burden.

In vain Father sought a suitable bride for his lonely son. At the beginning of the third year Father called to him the chief servant he had adopted and trusted with all he owned.

"You must make a long journey to find a kindhearted woman for my son. She must resist the ways of Shining-One and willingly walk with Garden-Maker."

"Where shall I find such a bride?"

"North at the City of Crossroads the children and grandchildren of my older brother graze their flocks and herds. Promise-Keeper will send an angel before you to prepare the way and you will find a bride."

The servant loaded ten camels with treasures and supplies. Then he traveled far to the north to the city where Merchant's family had first stopped on its long trek from the City of the Moon to the new land.

A cycle of the moon passed and the chief servant stood outside the City of Crossroads. He stopped near the public well as the sun sank low and watched the young girls giggle and gossip as they filled their clay jars with fresh water. Sitting in the shade of palm trees he dusted off his clothes and camels. Now at his destination, what should he do? How was he to find a kind-hearted bride willing to leave her family to walk with Promise-Keeper and marry a stranger? The sun fell lower. Father had taught him long ago to ask Promise-Keeper in moments of uncertainty.

"Please help me," begged the servant.

"What do you wish?" came the voice on the wind.

"Some sign that will direct me to a suitable bride."

"Tell me the sign and I will direct you."

"I will ask for a drink and if she treats me kindly, saying, 'I will pour water in the trough for your camels as well.' Then I will know she is the one."

As the servant looked toward the well, a beautiful woman with a large clay jar balanced gracefully on her shoulder glided toward him. The setting sun lit her face and her dark eyes sparkled. Black silky hair hung below her shoulders, framing a perfectly proportioned face made even more lovely by her warm smile. The servant was enraptured. She was as lovely as Princess had been so many years before.

"Please," he asked the passing young woman, "may I have a little water?"

She stopped to look into the weathered, sunburned face of the old man. "Surely." She lowered the heavy jar and gave him a drink. "I will pour water in the trough for your camels as well."

The servant stared in disbelief as she emptied her jar into the trough and returned to the well for more. The camels crowded around the trough and rapidly lapped up the cool refreshment. The servant could hardly contain his excitement. She had replied exactly as he had asked.

As the woman emptied her jar a third time, the servant pulled the leather bag from the lead camel and retrieved the carefully folded cloth. From its layers he uncovered thick golden bracelets and a ring of gold such as beautiful women of wealth wore in their pierced noses.

The young woman filled the jar again for her own needs and began to hurry off. "I am late and must be home by sunset."

"Wait a moment," said the servant. "I give you these gifts for your kindheartedness." He set the nose ring and bracelets in her hand.

She fingered the jewelry and said, "They are very expensive."

"And now they belong to you," said the servant as he slipped the bracelets onto her wrists. "Who is your family?"

"I live with my parents and brother. My great-grandfather was a powerful merchant in the City of the Moon. My grandfather moved here long ago."

"Do you have places where my men and I can stay the night?"

"Yes, and we have straw and feed for your camels. Let me ask my brother. I will be back soon to show you the way."

"I will wait," said the servant. As she hurried down the well-worn path, the servant looked toward the violet sky and whispered, "Garden-Maker, Promise-Keeper, you who live beyond the sky and hold the stars in your hands. Thank you for sending an angel before me to prepare my way."

The young woman rushed home but before she could say anything her brother saw her jewelry. "Where did you get these?" he asked.

"A man at the well gave them and asked if he might stay with us tonight."

"Where is he now?"

"At the well with his men and camels. I told him I would return."

Her brother walked with the woman to greet this visitor of obvious wealth with a warm embrace. "Your room is ready and there's plenty of food for your camels."

The camels were unloaded and fed. The servant and his companions washed and sat down to a much-welcomed dinner.

"Before we eat," proclaimed the servant, "I must tell you why we have come." The servant told of Father and the son and the search for a bride. He spoke of the journey north and his request that Promise-Keeper give him a sign.

"That is why you gave her such gifts?" asked the brother.

"The gifts are yours whatever you decide. If she does not accept, I understand. I would tell you one thing more. Your grandfather is Father's older brother."

"Your master is Merchant? This is very good," said the young woman's father, who had been silent. "If Promise-Keeper has chosen my daughter to be the bride, I would be a fool to stand in his way."

"What is your desire?" the servant asked the young woman.

"I will not question the ways of Promise-Keeper."

"Are you willing to follow the truth wherever it may take you?"

"Yes," responded the woman with steadfast confidence. "I'll go where Promise-Keeper leads and if he wants me as the bride, I will be the bride."

The servant asked his men to bring in gifts. They set a woolen blanket filled with jewelry and clothing of the finest thread before the young maiden. Gold and silver sparkled in the firelight.

"These are a token of the riches that await you in the new land," said the servant.

The future bride bent to her knees, amazed at the wealth before her—
bracelets and anklets and necklaces;
earrings and nose rings and rings for every finger;
pearls and emeralds and sapphires—
all glittering in overwhelming splendor. She shook her head in astonishment but then looked beneath the jewelry to dresses and robes and veils of colorful silks and linens. She carefully ran her hands over the material and held each to her body. Then she gasped. Underneath all was the most beautiful dress she had ever seen: dazzling white, like the sun reflecting on the purest of snow; sewn in elegant simplicity with silver thread and laced with small crystals which made the gown twinkle with a brightness that outshone the stars.

"For your marriage festival," said the servant. Another woolen blanket was carried in, filled with family gifts. Precious stones and carved ivory, rare spices and exotic perfumes, expensive clothing and many other impressive gifts.

"Tonight is a night to celebrate," said the bride-to-be's father. "My daughter has found a wealthy husband and we have found our family. Garden-Maker will surely bless this union and its children."

Early the next morning, before the heat had settled on the land, the bride's family bid farewell. Tears and hugs and words of wisdom were exchanged. Parting was not easy, but it was right. With sadness and excitement the bride and her servants mounted their kneeling camels. A firm prod and a tightening of the reins brought these lumbering animals clumsily to their feet. They took the dusty trail west and then south, following the curve of the fertile crescent.

Laughter lived in the southern part of the new land, near the Oasis of the Angel where Handmaiden first found comfort half a century before. But the son had grown restless and waited in the Valley of Apples for the homecoming of his father's servants. The servant had been gone almost three cycles of the moon and no word was heard.

"If he is gone any longer will that be a good or a bad sign?" asked the son. "What if he cannot find a bride?"

"Promise-Keeper sent an angel ahead to prepare the way," said Father. "Promise-Keeper will not fail you. My servant will return with a bride."

But the son remained impatient. He prepared his mother's tent to make it comfortable for his unseen bride. He tried to imagine how she would look and her manner. He asked Promise-Keeper to tell him the traits of a good husband. His anticipation grew, yet the servants still lingered beyond the valley. Would tomorrow be the day of the bride?

Shadows grew long and the air turned cool and Laughter strolled through his father's fields thinking how different life would be with a bride. As he lifted his eyes he saw a cloud of dust to the north. Someone was coming! He cut across the field toward the travelers, straining to identify them. Ten camels emerged from the brownish cloud, riders clung to eight wooden saddles. Could this be what he awaited? Some of the riders were in female dress. His heart beat faster and he restrained himself from running toward the travelers.

"Please stop," requested the bride as she pulled back on her reins. The servant halted the caravan and helped the young woman from her camel.

"Who is that man walking the field toward us?"

"By next week he will be your husband."

She watched her future husband walk through the dying light with his shy, yet determined, stride. He was a handsome man with a gentle look and a happy smile. She could tell he was kind and peaceful. She asked, "Is he a good man?"

"A very good man," said the chief servant.

"Will he love me?" she asked.

"He will cherish you."

"And I will cherish him," she said softly. Remembering the custom of the land and feeling dusty and unattractive, she veiled her face, stepped off the road and slowly walked across the open field toward the man with whom she would spend her life.

Soon began the week of wedding celebration. People came from as far as the City of Palms and the Oasis of the Angel. Nephew and his two daughters came from the oval plain to the east, and friends came from the hill country overlooking the Great Sea to the west. The son looked regal in a costly robe of bright colors bedecked with pieces of gold. The bride, whose face remained hidden, was breathtaking in her white dress and silver veil. Her jewelry was stunning and her elegance caught every eye.

Laughter watched the beautiful woman beside him for clues to her heart.

Her voice showed compassion.

Her words revealed conviction.

Her step betrayed boldness and confidence.

He tried to catch a glimpse of her face, but the veil kept her countenance hidden. He reminded himself that the heart was more important than appearance. When she noticed that he was watching, she placed her hand on his hand and a peace washed over him. This was right. If only Mother might see his happiness. His bride squeezed his hand and said, "I'm so glad Promise-Keeper brought us together."

The week was filled with eating and speeches, music and gift-giving. For six days Father hosted an elaborate banquet where everybody ate too much and for six nights the valley danced itself to sleep. On the seventh day the couple pledged their love and that night entered the bridal chamber where the silver veil fell to the floor and Laughter looked on the beautiful face of his beloved.

> TO WIN AT ANY COST
> PLANTS SEEDS OF RESENTMENT
> THAT EASILY GROW TO HATRED—
> TURNING BROTHERS AGAINST EACH OTHER.

❦

CHAPTER 10

THE TWINS

I'm so sorry," cried Bride. "I don't know what is wrong."

"I love you," said Laughter. "This is not your fault. My mother waited fifty years for my birth."

"I have failed you. Tomorrow I will go back to the City of Crossroads and you can break with me."

"I will not break with you or abandon you or hold this against you."

"But that is always done at the City of Crossroads. Besides, you must produce sons to fulfill the words of Promise-Keeper."

"Even if it were impossible for you to carry life, impossibilities have never stopped Promise-Keeper from keeping his word. When Promise-Keeper told my parents they would have a son, they laughed. I am the child of their laughter. Promise-Keeper has said that if I walk with him, he will walk with me. He led me high into the hills and told me all that will belong to our children. He promised my father and he promises me that my descendants will be as plentiful as the stars."

"Then I will be content," said Bride.

Years passed and a famine choked the land. The Oasis of the Angel turned the hue of dust. Flocks fell over and herds grew gaunt. Laughter walked with Promise-Keeper and spoke of the Land of Deltas.

"Trust me," said Promise-Keeper. "Stay in the land I have given to you and your descendants. Take your cattle and flocks north to the hills near the Great Sea where your father lived."

The son listened and obeyed. He moved all his flocks and herds two days northwest to the same dry streambed beside which his father had

135

pitched his tent. Here Laughter planted crops and found water in the wells his father had dug long ago. His crops produced an amazing yield and his livestock multiplied. He was so prosperous that the sea people became jealous and conflicts broke out. So Laughter moved on. In time the famine ended and he returned to the Oasis of the Angel.

For twenty years the son prayed for a son and for twenty years Bride did not carry life. His aged father remarried and had six sons. The son cried out to Promise-Keeper, "Why is my father blessed sixfold when he is old and has no need for an heir, yet I pray every night for one son and am left childless? Do you care about my pain? Do you listen to my cries?"

"I care and listen and act when the time is right," said Promise-Keeper. "The time has come even now and your wife is carrying life. This morning she felt the movement of her sons."

"Sons?"

"Two wrestle in Bride's womb and they will continue to wrestle long after they have broken free."

So after twenty summers of marriage Bride was carrying life and six cycles of the moon later she gave birth to two sons as Promise-Keeper had said. When they were born the first had a reddish hue with hairy skin and was called Red. The second tried to push past his brother to see the light first, so he was called Schemer. On their eighth day Laughter carried both infants to a field near the oasis and with a sharp blade gave them each the cut of commitment as Father had cut him sixty years before.

The battle between Red and Schemer continued. They so differed that they could not agree on any subject. Red was rough and rugged;
he preferred to be alone
and hiked the hills with bow slung over his shoulder.
While Schemer
was refined and friendly;
he shared conversation with all
and stayed at home to help his mother with daily chores.

So his bride grew close to Schemer, while Laughter favored Red, his strong eldest son. Such favoritism only fueled frustration between the twins, but their conflicts were kept under control in the presence of their parents.

The boys were young men of fifteen when news arrived from the Valley of Apples that Father's spirit had moved beyond the blue planet.

Laughter and his bride traveled north to bury Father. On the western slopes of the beautiful valley, Mother's son and Handmaiden's son met without animosity. They hugged and wept and carried their father's body through the circular opening into the dim light of the burial cave. They placed his body near Mother.

"Now they can walk together with Promise-Keeper beyond the sky," said Laughter.

"And with all the ancient ones," said his half-brother. "He can speak with Man about the garden and Walker about the world and Builder about the boat. He loved to watch for rainbows and remind us of their message that no matter how distant he seems, Promise-Keeper is always close and he will always care."

Outside the cave the two men said their sad good-byes and went their ways. Both knew their progeny would be great. Both sensed that blood would be shed between their family lines and that if Father knew the future sorrow would pierce his heart.

At the Oasis of the Angel Red and Schemer enjoyed the time without their parents. Red grabbed his bow and headed for the wide open fields in search of deer or lions. Schemer hung about the tents and learned from the elders. Hunting did not go well for Red and he found no food to sustain him. He came home empty-handed and exhausted and weakened by hunger.

"Schemer, please give me something to eat. I have endured days without food."

"But I made only enough soup for myself."

"Then give me bread?"

"There is only the one loaf I am eating with my soup."

"I need something to eat—anything!"

"There's nothing here but my soup and bread."

"I will do whatever you want for just a little soup. Please."

"Whatever I want?" pondered Schemer with a sly smile. "You have nothing I want. . .except your birthright. Are you desperate enough to trade your birthright for soup?"

"But that is the double inheritance. You would receive two-thirds of the wealth. A birthright is worth much, much more than a bowl of soup."

"Unless you are starving."

"Give me the soup," said Red. "I swear before Promise-Keeper to give you the double inheritance of my birthright."

Schemer brought the soup and bread, hardly believing his good fortune. A snake hissed behind a nearby rock as Red devoured his expensive meal. Then he threw the clay bowl to the ground, shattering it into a dozen sharp fragments. "I hate you and I hate my birthright." With that he stood up and spat in his brother's face and vanished into the open fields to the south.

Years passed and the twins became men. Red grew ever closer to his father and Schemer nearer to his mother. On his travels Red met the people of the land and saw two women he desired. He married both, though they followed the ways of Shining-One. Soon they pulled Red further and further from Promise-Keeper. Schemer listened to the elders and learned the ways of Promise-Keeper. He said he wished to follow the one beyond the sky, but dawn came too early.

Laughter became old and cataracts clouded and then blinded his eyes. One morning he awoke with a heaviness in his chest and thought his days on the blue planet were near their end. He called his favorite son into his tent.

"You've lost your birthright, but I can still give you the blessing of the first-born. Before I die I would enjoy venison once more. Get your bow and go hunting. Bring back a deer and cook it with the spices I like. Then I will bless you."

"I will be back soon," said the hunter as he left the tent. Within minutes Red had his bow over his shoulder and was headed east from the oasis with his eye searching the open fields for game.

Bride had been outside her husband's tent making bread and had overheard this conversation. So as soon as Red was gone she called her favorite son. "Your father will give your brother his blessing today. Perhaps there is a way for you to gain the blessing."

"But how?"

"It will take Red time to stalk his game. Run to the flocks and kill two of the best kids. I will fix them with enough onions and spices that he will not notice that his food is not venison."

"But Father will know I am not Red."

"If you dress in Red's clothes and make your arms hairy and give your

skin an outdoor smell and mimic the words of your brother you will succeed, for Father's eyes are not as clear as they once were. If he recognizes
you, I will accept his anger."

So Schemer did what his mother instructed. He covered the back of
his hands with hairy animal skins and took his father's favorite meal to him.

"Here is your meal," Schemer said as he set the meal before Laughter.

"Is that you, Schemer?"

"No, it is Red," mumbled Schemer. "Enjoy your meal then give me
your blessing."

"How did you kill and dress and cook your game so quickly?"

"Promise-Keeper directed my way and aimed my arrow."

"Come closer and let me place my hand on yours."

Schemer moved close and his father touched his hand. "Your voice
sounds like Schemer, but these are the hands of Red."

The old man ate his meal and drank some wine. Then he wiped his
lips and said, "Now come close."

Schemer bowed before his father and his father kissed him. As he did
so the scent of Red's clothes—the wild smell of the open fields—caught his
father's nose and convinced him that this was Red. He placed his feeble
hands on his son's head.

"May Promise-Keeper grant you all you need from beyond the sky
and upon this planet. May you be a leader above all leaders, even over your
own brother. May those who stand against you be defeated and those who
stand with you be honored."

His father kissed his cheek again and Schemer rose. The two
embraced and Schemer left. Soon Red came to his father with the venison
he had prepared and a skin of fine wine.

"What?" said Father, his voice strained in agitation. "Who is this?"

"I am Red, your eldest son." He moved close so that his father smelled
his clothes and felt his hand and listened to his voice.

The old man's face paled and his body trembled.

"Schemer has deceived me. I have given him your blessing."

Red let out a heart-wrenching scream as he heaved the steak against the
wall and threw the wineskin to the ground, splattering himself and his father.
"How could this happen? Can you give me no blessing? Schemer has stolen
my birthright and today he took my blessing. Is there nothing you can do?"

"I have made him wealthy and you his servant."

"Do something for my protection or he will destroy me."

"Bow before me to receive the blessing that remains." Red bowed before his father as had Schemer. His father kissed him on the cheek and spoke, "May Promise-Keeper grant you sustenance and survival in a good land. May you be a warrior with a swift sword. Though you must submit to your brother, may Promise-Keeper defend you against injustice. May you grow strong and restless until you break your brother's hold."

The anger of Red clamped his jaw and set his heart ablaze. That evening he saw his brother walking through the camp and followed him. There would have been blows had Schemer not seen his brother's intent and fled.

"You can't run forever, thief," Red yelled. He removed the bow from his shoulder and pulled back the string and sighted his straightest arrow. "My arrow can cut down the quickest game."

Schemer stopped and stared down his brother's shaft. "Father will not forgive you if you kill me."

"I am not so sure of that," said Red as he loosened the tension on his bow. "But Father's days are short and you will quickly follow him to the grave. I will track you down whereever you are and drive my arrow through your heart. You will die at my hand and I will be avenged on that day."

Red placed the arrow back into his quiver and slung the bow over his shoulder and turned his back on his twin brother. Then he disappeared into the open hills he loved so well.

ONE MAY ESCAPE
HOME OR PEOPLE OR DANGER.
BUT ONE NEVER ESCAPES
CONSEQUENCES.

CHAPTER 11

THE ESCAPE

Y ou must leave before your brother kills you," said Bride.

"But where? Red says he will track me down wherever I go."

"North to the City of Crossroads. My brother will protect you and give you work. When Red has forgotten his threat I will send word that you can return. I will speak with your father."

Bride turned and went into her husband's tent. She lay down beside him and ran her hands across his chest. "Promise-Keeper gave your blessing to Schemer for a reason."

"It had nothing to do with Promise-Keeper," murmured Laughter in anger. "Schemer tricked me and lied to me."

"Promise-Keeper could have shown you the truth before you gave the blessing."

"But he didn't."

"No, he didn't," said Bride. "Maybe Promise-Keeper rejects Red because he married people who follow the ways of Shining-One. Perhaps he wants the bloodline of his people to be pure. You are Father's son and I am from his brother's line. If we send Schemer to my brother at the City of Crossroads, he can marry one of his cousins and the bloodline will remain true among our kinsmen."

The old man nodded. "I will send Schemer north."

Early the next morning after his walk with Promise-Keeper, Laughter called Schemer to his tent. "Your actions have caused much trouble, but I still love you."

"Forgive my deception. I was wrong and now Red will take my life."

"Promise-Keeper can make something good from your wrong. Your mother and I want you to marry a kindhearted woman. We are concerned that you will be tempted as your brother to marry a follower of Shining-One. So we are sending you north to find a wife who knows Promise-Keeper."

"How will I find the right one?"

"Promise-Keeper sent an angel before the servant of my father, and he found my bride. If we ask, he will do the same for you."

"Why should he care about me?" asked Schemer. "I believe in him and in all the old stories, but I've never walked with him."

"Someday you will, for you hold his promises in your birthright and blessing. Meanwhile you have a journey before you. At its end you will find a kindhearted woman and have many children. Just as Promise-Keeper blessed my father and he blessed me, soon he will bless you. He will give you all the land around us and descendants as plentiful as the stars."

Schemer hugged his father and said, "Thank you." Then he loaded his provisions on a camel and headed north.

When Red heard that his father had sent Schemer north to find a good woman, he burned with rage. "I've lost my birthright and my blessing and now my father's respect. I will also choose a wife related to his father." Red went east into the great desert to find his father's half-brother, Handmaiden's son. Red asked to marry one of his daughters. Consent was given and the couple wed; but Red's parents were no more happy with this union than with his other wives.

Riding his camel north, Schemer kept off the main roads and constantly looked behind. He would give his brother no opportunity to send an arrow through his chest. He stopped one night at a rocky spot a day north of the City of Palms. From this high ground between the Winding River and the Great Sea he could see anyone's approach far in all directions.

He lay and watched the night sky. As his eyes grew heavy the stars seemed to move and change shapes. Schemer rubbed away the sleep. Each star seemed to sparkle and its rays lengthen. They came alive and cold stars became moving creatures. Long, golden hair framed brilliant countenances and thousands of white-hot feet strolled across infinity. Some of these beautiful beings moved toward him, while others moved away. Angel after angel climbed and descended a massive silver staircase that stretched from the blue planet to beyond the sky.

Suddenly brilliant starlight shone upon the stair, piercing the night of the blue planet. "I am Garden-Maker and Promise-Keeper," announced a powerful voice amid the radiance. . . .

"I walk with your father.

"I have walked with your father's father.

"I long to walk with you."

"Why have you come to me in my dreams?" asked Schemer.

"Because you don't always listen when you're awake. But now you must hear, for I want to give you the promise I gave your father and his father. I will give descendants to you as plentiful as the stars and I will give them all the land as far as you can see."

"What will become of the promises if my brother takes my life?"

"I will be your shield and will protect you wherever you go. And when the time is right I will bring you back to this land. I am always true to my word." As the final phrase echoed through the night, the brightest star faded and the silver staircase disappeared and the angels shrank into tiny sparks on night's black canopy.

As the sun chased the stars from the sky, Schemer walked the ridge amazed. "The majesty of Promise-Keeper's presence in this place overwhelms me. It's a portal to the infinite universe beyond. Promise-Keeper is more than I ever imagined. All I have heard about him must be true.

"Promise-Keeper," he called to the sky. "You've opened my eyes and let me see a deeper truth. If you preserve me in this difficulty and bring me back safely to my father's house, I will walk with you each morning as did my father and his father."

Schemer set up a stone marker as a reminder of what he had seen and heard. Suddenly a breeze blew in from the west and whirled around the monument. Schemer stepped back as the wind howled with unmistakable articulation: "I will be your shield and will protect you wherever you go."

About twenty days later he arrived at a field near the City of Crossroads where a small group of men with their flocks of sheep waited. In the center of the field was a private well with a large covering stone. When the flocks had gathered, the men would roll away the stone and water the sheep and then return the stone to its place. Schemer asked the men, "Do you know Bride's brother?"

"He is one of the wealthiest of landowners. And here comes one of his daughters."

Schemer's eyes followed to where the man pointed. There, coming his way, was one of the most beautiful maidens he had ever seen. With a staff in her hand and the breeze blowing her hair, she led her sheep into the field and approached the men.

"And who is the stranger?" the shepherdess asked.

"I am your cousin," said Schemer, "the son of Bride. And I have come to water your flocks." Before the maiden could respond he rolled away the stone with his powerful arms and drew water for her sheep.

"Why have you come?" she asked when he finished.

"I am looking for my uncle."

"Watch my sheep and I will return with him."

Watching her hurry away, the first seeds of love were planted. He addressed his feelings to the sheep. "Promise-Keeper has indeed sent an angel before me to prepare the way. And I will be surprised if your shepherdess does not one day become my bride."

His uncle rushed to greet him warmly. "My house is yours. Come stay with me as long as you wish." So for the next month Schemer stayed with his uncle—

he tended his flocks;

he fought off wolves;

he birthed lambs and kids;

and he fell deeply in love with the maiden shepherdess. At the end of the month his uncle approached him and said, "You are a good worker and I want you to stay. What can I pay you?"

"I don't want your money, but I will gladly work seven years to marry your daughter."

Bride's brother had two unmarried daughters, and the shepherdess was the younger. Custom decreed that the older marry first. But in seven years she would certainly have found a husband.

But seven years later the older daughter was still unmarried. The brother also knew that once Schemer had the hand of the shepherdess his free labor would end. There was a way to solve both problems.

The wedding of Schemer and Shepherdess occasioned a week of ecstatic celebration. On the last day an extravagant banquet was eaten and the sacred vows exchanged. Schemer drank much wine during the day and as he stood before his veiled bride he noticed nothing amiss. That night the bridal chamber was dark and all seemed perfect as she slipped away her veils and fell into her husband's arms. So the morning sun brought a shock when Schemer saw who slept beside him—his bride's older sister.

But now the older sister was his bride.

He rushed to confront his father-in-law. "You know I worked these years for Shepherdess."

"My older daughter is also a fine woman," said Father-in-Law.

"You know I love your younger daughter and would do anything for her, but you have cheated me."

"By custom my younger daughter cannot marry before the elder. You have a wife now and you cannot abandon her. But you can marry my younger daughter as well. Let us extend our agreement another seven years."

"Give me the one I love and I will work another seven years."

Schemer soon learned that he had married sisters who competed with one another—almost as intensely as he and Red. Older Sister first had children, so Shepherdess gave Schemer her handmaiden. The elder did the same. By fourteen summers of labor the perplexed man had eleven children by four rival women. His was a family marked by jealousy and argument and confusion.

Schemer went to his father-in-law. "The time has come to part I have been here much longer than I intended and I hunger for the land of my birth."

"Don't go," begged Father-in-Law. "While you have worked with my flocks and herds Promise-Keeper has given me great success. Tell me your price to stay."

"I must gather my own flocks and herds."

"You can build up your livestock and continue to build up mine. Ask what you want and it will be yours."

Here was the offer Schemer had hoped to hear. "I ask little," he said. "I will stay for all your multicolored sheep and goats, and the black lambs. And while I work for you, any of these born will be mine."

This man is a fool, thought Father-in-Law happily, *for those are the rarest markings.*

The two sealed their agreement with a feast. They were both joyful, for each thought he had outsmarted the other. After Schemer left, his father-in-law told his sons to quickly separate out the multicolored sheep and goats, and any of the black lambs. They would drive them three days toward the setting sun—and hide them.

"But Schemer will notice some of the animals are missing."

"They might have died. He cannot accuse us unless he finds them."

When Schemer went out to count the multicolored sheep and goats and black lambs, there were none. But he said nothing. His discerning eye had noticed what lambs would look like when certain sheep mated. And he looked to Promise-Keeper for blessing. Soon his flocks abounded with multicolored and black offspring. Then he bred the strongest animals with his multicolored stock and his flocks multiplied with animals of such quality that his father-in-law burned with envy.

Schemer overheard the sons of his father-in-law complaining. "Somehow, Schemer is stealing our inheritance. We must act quickly or he will take all we have."

He immediately went to his father-in-law. "Your sons are angry and plot against me."

The response was cool. "I can't stop them, and I agree that you are taking from us. There should not be so many multicolored animals and the multicolored should not be so much stronger. Tomorrow I go west to do shearing. You resolve your dispute with my sons."

"What flocks do you have to the west?" asked Schemer with feigned surprise. "You have never mentioned them."

"I have only now bought them," Father-in-Law lied with unconvincing nervousness. "Must I tell you everything?"

Schemer walked away discouraged. Looking beyond the sky he cried out, "Promise-Keeper, what should I do? I am no longer welcome in the land of my wives."

A strong northerly gust pushed him southward. "It is time to return to the land I have promised. Return to the place of the portal. Remember your vow: 'If you preserve me in this difficulty and bring me back safely to my father's house, I will walk with you each morning as did my father and his father.' "

"I remember my vow," said Schemer, "but I am surrounded by brothers-in-law who wish to harm me and back home is a brother who wants to kill me."

"Follow me and you will be safe," said Promise-Keeper.

He spoke to his wives of his danger and Promise-Keeper's order to leave. Both wives listened carefully and agreed that if Promise-Keeper said to go, they must go. . . . "But our father and brothers will stop us."

"We will wait until your father is some distance away. Then we will leave in the darkness. When he finds we are gone it will be too late."

Father-in-Law and his sons headed west. Two days later during a moonless night, Schemer, his wives, his children, the servants and all his livestock quietly moved southward. Before they left, Shepherdess stole the valuable superstitious charms that her father thought brought him luck. His family outwardly followed Promise-Keeper, but they dabbled in things that Promise-Keeper hated. "Father will be furious no matter what we do," she told her sister. "These will help us bargain if he tries to stop us."

Three days later Father-in-Law heard of Schemer's escape. One of his servants ran from the city to the place of shearing with the report, "Your son-in-law has taken your daughters, your grandchildren and all his flocks. They disappeared in the middle of the night and it looks like they're moving toward the land of Schemer's birth."

By the time the servant was finished his master was trembling with rage. "Schemer can't do this to me. I want my flocks back and my daughters back and their children."

"There is something else," said the servant. "Schemer also took your charms."

"Gather every one of my servants and anyone who owes me a favor. Tell them to bring their sharpest weapons and mount their fastest animals. We will chase that thief down."

Father-in-Law and his men pursued Schemer hundreds of miles. South of the City of Caravans and east of the Winding River, they entered a rough, hilly land with thick forests. They knew they would find him, for his sheep and goats could not move quickly. On the seventh day, Father-in-Law crossed a ridge and saw fires burning in the valley below. His scouts confirmed that they had found Schemer's camp. Gathering his men, Father-in-Law planned a dawn attack. "Don't hurt my daughters or their children, but if anyone else raises a sword, cut them down. Most important, find my good-luck charms. By the time the sun touches its highest point in the sky I want the charms and Schemer at my feet."

"Do you want your son-in-law alive?" asked one of his men.

Father-in-Law stared into the darkness for a moment. "I really don't care."

ESCAPES TAKE ONE ONLY SO FAR,
FOR SOONER OR LATER
ONE MUST TURN TO FACE
WHAT ONE'S RUNNING FROM.

CHAPTER 12

THE RETURN

B e careful," boomed a voice across the universe, "or you will answer to me."

Father-in-Law sat up on his sleeping mat and frantically looked around. All was dark and the hills were quiet. He laid down his head and closed his eyes.

"I am Schemer's shield and he is my chosen one," the voice boomed once more. "I have sent my angels to protect him and bring him back to the place of the portal."

Suddenly a giant angel stood before Father-in-Law. His rugged face glowed while his piercing blue eyes twinkled like the stars. He stood stern and silent. Strapped to his left arm was a full-length shield and clutched in his right hand was a golden sword. He swung it with a flaming blur that left phosphorescent tracers in the night air.

As Father-in-Law peered deeply into his dream the booming voice of Promise-Keeper returned, "Anyone who stands against my chosen one will be defeated and anyone who stands with him will be honored."

A bright internal flash sliced through his slumber and the angel disappeared. Father-in-Law awakened his makeshift army, which was soon to attack the camp of his son-in-law, Schemer. "Don't harm Schemer," he ordered. "No matter what he does, I don't want the slightest bruise or the faintest blood spot on him. Treat him kindly and with utmost respect. Enter his camp with your swords in their sheaths and tell him that I wish to speak with him."

Several hours later Father-in-Law stared into Schemer's face and asked, "Why have you done this to me? Why did you sneak away in the middle of the night with my daughters and their children? Why did you steal my good-luck charms?"

Schemer unflinchingly returned Father-in-Law's stare. "I slipped away because I do not trust you. As for your charms, I have no use for them."

"My servants say you stole them."

"I give you my word that I did not take anything of yours. Search my camp and if they find anything that belongs to you, the person who has it will be put to death."

Father-in-Law's men thoroughly searched but found nothing. When they returned, Schemer confronted his father-in-law. "You have chased me like an unruly thief to the northern boundary of the new land and you have no charge against me."

"You took my daughters and my grandchildren and my flocks."

"I have purchased all of those things with patience and hard labor. You can make no claim that these are yours. Yet you were willing to kill me and drag my wives and possessions back to the City of Crossroads. Who acts as a thief here?"

The old man bowed his head in shame, but then looked Schemer in the eye. "What you say may be just, but I still don't trust you."

"Nor I you, but let us stop this enmity."

So Schemer set a large stone upright in the ground. "Let this be a boundary marker between your territory and mine. Since neither of us trust the other, let us promise not to cross this point. I will stay to the south and you to the north."

"May Promise-Keeper be our judge," said Father-in-Law.

The two men ate together to seal their promise. Early the next morning Father-in-Law kissed his daughters and grandchildren, then he faced north. Schemer and his family faced south. Both men were true to their word and neither crossed the line. Neither did their children nor their children's children.

As Schemer moved over wooded hills, he caught flashes of silver around him. Glowing celestial forms followed on both sides, merging with brightness and shadows, here for a blink and then gone. His wives and children saw nothing but sunbeams dancing between pines and oaks. Yet Schemer knew that Promise-Keeper was keeping him safe.

When Schemer reached the Falling River he set up camp and sent messengers five days south to find his brother. "When you meet Red tell him I have been up north with our uncle and have done very well, but I miss my homeland and return peacefully as his humble servant."

A week later the messengers returned with news that Red was coming north with four hundred men to meet his twin.

"Four hundred?" Schemer's face went ashen as his dark eyes took on a hunted look. "He said he would hunt me down. I can't fight so many men." He looked beyond the sky and cried out, "Protect me. Shield me and my family from my brother's deadly aim. Bring me home safely and I will walk with you."

Suddenly the wind howled through the trees, "I am your shield and my angels walk on both sides of you, protecting your every step."

Schemer lifted his eyes to the surrounding hills and between the trees saw the silver twinkle of a thousand stars with a thousand shields and a thousand swords. He smiled and said, "Our lives are in Promise-Keeper's hands."

The next morning Schemer set apart livestock as a gift to soften his brother's heart.

Schemer sent three groups of animals across the Falling River toward the advancing forces of his twin. More than two hundred goats were followed by more than two hundred sheep and then a smaller group of camels and cattle and donkeys. The servants of each group were told to say to Red, "These are a gift from your humble brother who comes to make peace."

Schemer watched his animals fade into the distance and whispered beneath his breath, "I hope this works; I really hope this works." He moved the rest of his people and animals across the river. When all were settled for the night and the campfires were burning bright, he quietly crossed back to the north side of the river so he could be alone to think.

"I have been watching you," came a strong voice out of the darkness.

"Who are you? What do you want?" asked Schemer as he peered into the forest.

"I come to do battle with you," returned the voice.

"Are you a coward lying in ambush or will you show your face?"

The underbrush moved behind him and Schemer swung around to face a large man who glowed with the brilliance of an angel. The full moon shone on his lean face. He was serious and muscular with a full-length shield strapped to his left arm and a golden sword tight in his opposite hand. "I am here," he said with a quietly menacing air.

"I have no shield and sword."

The angel unstrapped his protection and dropped his weapon. "Why did you cross the river again?"

"I had much to consider."

"Like how to prepare for death?" the angel said with a sadness in his voice. "Why don't you trust Promise-Keeper?"

"I'm not sure. . . ."

"He has shown you a thousand swords hidden in the hills and still you doubt? Dear Schemer, when will you learn that success and safety do not rest upon your clever strategies? Promise-Keeper said he will be your shield."

"I have not learned trust," Schemer admitted.

"Then walk with him as your father and as his father."

"I will walk with him when he has brought me home safely."

"Will you truly, when you do not trust him?"

"Trust is not always easy," said Schemer, "when the world is full of danger and darkness and deceit."

"Do you believe Promise-Keeper lives beyond the sky and holds the stars in his hands? Do you believe Promise-Keeper is infinite and eternal and all-powerful?"

"Yes."

"Then the time has come to trust him."

"I'm not ready yet."

"We will see about that," said the angel as he stepped toward Schemer. Through the night the two wrestled. The angel would pin the man and ask, "Will you trust Promise-Keeper?" Each time Schemer somehow escaped and responded, "I'm not ready."

Finally the angel said, "When a lamb keeps wandering off the shepherd sometimes breaks the leg to make it dependent. Little lamb, if you truly wish to walk alone for now, that is your choice, but each step will be painful." And the angel reached down and twisted Schemer's hip from its joint. Pain shot through Schemer.

As the first rays of morning touched the eastern sky, Schemer threw himself forward with his good leg and locked his arms around the angel's middle. "I cannot beat you, but I can hold on to you until you give me what I want."

"Our battle is over."

"I refuse to let go until you bless me."

The angel tried to shake the man free, but Schemer held on with all his might.

"Your determination is mighty," laughed the angel. "Today you have a new name. You shall no longer be Schemer, for your days of scheming are coming to an end. Now you shall be known as Wrestler. You have spent your life wrestling against Promise-Keeper. Every morning he called your name and every morning you turned your back. But your trust is growing and from this time forward you will wrestle to pull closer, not away. You will find your peace. Then you will walk freely each morning, not just because of your vow but because you've learned to let go."

Schemer loosened his grip and thanked the angel. Then he let go and something deep inside felt good—very good.

The angel smiled as he picked up his shield and sword. He pointed south across the Falling River and said, "You are needed." Then he turned away and faded into the misty morning forest.

Wrestler saw a large army in the distance coming toward his camp, a strong bowman boldly walking at the front. He rushed forward but the pain of his twisted hip slowed him. He ignored the excruciating throb and forced himself across the river. Then he slowly walked forward, eyes on his enemy-brother, mind poised for the worst. His sweaty hand tightened on the hilt of his freshly sharpened sword.

Suddenly Red let out a loud yell and ran full-force toward his twin, four hundred men close on his heels.

Wrestler stopped.

He steadied himself and relaxed the grip on his sword.

He slowly lowered his body until his face touched the ground.

Seven times he bowed to the south. The road rumbled with eight hundred feet and the air screamed with the deafening roar of the advancing army. Wrestler lifted himself slowly to his feet and jammed the point of his sword into the earth. He stared into his brother's approaching eyes and prepared for death.

But at the moment before Wrestler expected his final breath, Red tossed down his bow and sword, threw open his hairy arms and wrapped them around his brother. His powerful hug lifted his twin off the ground. He swung him around as tears streamed down both of their faces. Then Red kissed Wrestler on the cheek and shouted, "Oh, how I've missed you."

Four hundred men encircled the two with joyous cheers and wild applause.

"I have wronged you," said Wrestler.

"That was long ago. Let us forgive the past of our youth. Let us begin again as men."

Wrestler's wives and children pushed through the crowd when they saw that everything was safe.

"Are all these little ones yours?" asked Red.

"Yes, Promise-Keeper has been gracious to me." Wrestler introduced his wives and children to his twin. Everybody gathered around—talking and laughing and hugging.

"Father said you would return with many children."

"How are our father and mother?" asked Wrestler fearfully.

"Father always thinks he's about to die, but he has a strong heart. He still lives in the Valley of the Apples." Then Red paused and looked at the ground. "Mother left the blue planet several years ago. Her bones lie beside our father's parents."

The two embraced again and then sat down to a festive meal. After the food was eaten and twenty years of life reviewed, Red headed south to his home. Wrestler turned due west, crossed the Winding River and traveled a day farther to a high ridge. Here Father had pitched his tent when he first came to the new land, before the famine drove him south to the Land of Deltas. Wrestler and his family settled deep in the hills where the pastures were green and the soil rich. For a hundred pieces of silver he bought land a short journey north of the place of the portal. Here Wrestler pitched his tent and built a simple stone altar on an isolated hilltop. Walking through his flocks he chose the most perfect of all newborn lambs and sacrificed it to Promise-Keeper.

As the smoke rose, Wrestler whispered to the wind, "The time has come to trust the one who lives beyond the sky and holds the stars in his hands."

The wind swirled around the altar and blew the smoke into Wrestler's face. He heard Promise-Keeper's voice: "If you are ready to walk, wash away any hint of Shining-One from you and your family and your servants. Then meet me at the place of the portal."

That evening Wrestler spoke to his family and servants, "You who have good-luck charms or symbols of Shining-One, give them to me now. We are the people of Promise-Keeper." Servants and family members solemnly searched their belongings and found their charms. They nearly filled a large woolen bag with talismans and amulets and zodiac images. Included were Father-in-Law's charms that Shepherdess had stolen. Wrestler's hip already seemed less painful as he journeyed to a lonely spot far from camp and buried the wicked bag in a deep hole at the base of a great oak.

Wrestler led his family and servants south to the place of the portal where he built an altar and told them the story of the angels on the silver staircase. Then he looked up beyond the sky and spoke to Promise-Keeper. "On this ground I vowed that if you brought me home safely I would walk with you. You have kept your word and now I will keep mine. Every morning as the sun colors the eastern sky I will walk with you as did my father and his father. I will trust you for you are my shield. Where you lead I will follow."

With an overwhelming sense of peace, Wrestler sacrificed a spotless newborn lamb as a token of ultimate gratitude. The Promise-Keeper looked down from beyond the sky and smiled. His voice echoed across the universe, "You have wrestled with me and found peace. You will have descendants as plentiful as the stars. You will produce a great nation with powerful kings. And all the land for as far as you can see will someday be yours."

As the smoke from the altar curled upward, clouds drifted across the blue sky and a warm sprinkle dampened the land. Wrestler looked up as the sun cut through the rain with the most beautiful of rainbows.

What had Garden-Maker said to Builder so long ago? Wrestler paused for a moment. Oh, yes. . ."no matter how distant I may seem, I am always close and I will always care."

PAST AND FUTURE EXIST SIDE BY SIDE;
SOME PEOPLE LIVE IN ONE,
SOME DREAM OF THE OTHER.

CHAPTER 13

THE DREAMER

Of his eleven sons, Wrestler favored one above the others. Special One was the youngest, the only child of Shepherdess. Now he stood beside his father and watched the sky. "Where do all the colors come from?"

"From the imagination of Promise-Keeper."

"Why does he paint on the sky?" asked the six-year-old.

"To make us stop and look up. Sometimes people get so busy they forget about Promise-Keeper."

"Have you ever forgotten about him?"

"Yes," said Wrestler, "but no more. Every morning I walk with him."

"Can I walk with him, too?"

"You're very small. The walks are not easy and you will become tired."

"You said he lives beyond the sky and holds the stars in his hands. Is that true?"

"Yes."

"Then Promise-Keeper can carry me."

"Meet me here tomorrow morning, just before the sun first touches the eastern sky."

"Thank you," said the boy as he hugged his father. "I'll be here."

And he was. Every morning thereafter he arose before the day and walked beside his father. Together they met Promise-Keeper in the lustrous half-light and walked the ridges and valleys of the new land. The old and the young laughed and shared their hearts with the one who knew all. Soon the ten older brothers saw what the favorite was doing. They were jealous but not one of them got up early to join the walk.

As the moon passed through its cycles, Shepherdess grew round with a new life within her. Before her second child was born all the family was to travel two days south to the Valley of Apples. Here they would settle to care for Wrestler's father in his old age. The caravan moved slowly along the main road—there was no need to hurry—and the weary mother appreciated the easygoing pace. Her husband had built a comfortable wagon for the journey, balanced on tightly pegged wooden wheels and pulled by a sturdy, plodding pair of oxen. The floor was covered by a thick bed of the softest uncombed wool to cushion her from the bumps and ruts of the road. The roof was stretched with coarse cotton fabric to shelter her from the pounding sun and the sides were left open to allow in any fresh breeze. Her husband's deep love for her showed through his careful craftsmanship.

The mother-to-be dipped a strip of cloth into a clay jar of water to dampen her forehead.

"Let me do that," said her handmaiden who took the cloth and gently pressed it against her skin. The sweat slipped down her face and her body ached. A sharp pain shot through her abdomen and stole her breath. She gasped for air, eyes wide with panic and arms wild with action.

"What is wrong?" asked the handmaiden urgently.

"I don't know," she groaned. "It hurts so bad."

The handmaiden tenderly rubbed the sore spot until the pains subsided. The mother-to-be closed her eyes in exhaustion. Could this be some form of birth pain? No, it was different—

more intense,

more disorienting,

more frightening.

She breathed deeply and everything felt better, at least for a moment.

She held her stomach and felt the baby push hard against her bladder. The excitement of life stirring within her brought a smile. But why was she so tired? And why the bolts of pain? She'd never felt these during her first pregnancy. The baby moved again. At least her child was alive and active.

The next day as the sun climbed high, the pain grew deeper and more consuming. She gritted her teeth and tried to restrain the tears, but the pain increased to an excruciating level. A shrill cry escaped her trembling lips, bringing everybody within hearing to an abrupt stop.

In a moment Wrestler was at her side. She groaned and gasped. Her skin was colorless and her eyes rolled without vision. The soft mattress beneath her back absorbed the shocking scarlet of her limp body. Wrestler carefully placed his hand behind her neck and brought a cup of cool water to her faded lips.

"Get the midwife," he yelled to the curious crowd of onlookers. "We are having a baby." Turning back to his wife, he held her hand as a violent contraction shook her, stealing what little strength she had left.

She choked on the water and flung her arms back in anguish. "Help me," she squeaked almost inaudibly. Wrestler bent close and stroked her tangled hair.

"The midwife is coming."

"I can see angels—thousands of them—walking up and down the silver staircase. Good-bye, my dear," she said in a faltering voice.

"You can't leave me."

"The angels are lifting me. Take care of Special One and. . ." she faded and then returned. "Save my baby."

"I will." He squeezed her hand as her pulse weakened. "I promise I will."

A moment later the midwife delivered a loud and healthy son. As one life filled his lungs with a sturdy cry and saw the brightness of the blue planet for the first time, another life emptied her lungs with a final whimper and watched the colors grow dim. She would not cuddle or nurse her secondborn. Before she could see the tiny face, the vividness of another dimension broke through, lifting her from her body and transporting her beyond the sky to the majestic feet of Promise-Keeper.

Wrestler held the infant close to his chest as silent tears streamed down his weathered face. He gently closed his beloved's eyes and kissed her tenderly.

"Why does Mother lay so still?" asked Special One.

"Her spirit has gone to live with Promise-Keeper," said Wrestler as he wiped the wetness from his eyes.

"When will she come back?"

"She will not come back, my son."

The boy hung his head. "Is she angry at me?"

"Oh, no! You were her greatest joy."

"Then why did she leave us?"

"It was time for her to move beyond the blue planet. Some day we will walk the infinite skies and see her once again."

Near the road they buried her in a peaceful field of grass near the Village of Hope, a few hours' walk south of the City of Palms. Several days later the caravan entered the Valley of Apples, that fertile paradise where his father and his father's father had pitched their tents and walked with Promise-Keeper. Wrestler and his sons were welcomed by an old man he had not seen in over twenty years. The two hugged and the old man said, "It's good to have you home."

For ten summers Wrestler lived in prosperity in the Valley of Apples. Together he and his father watched twelve sons grow in knowledge and stature. Yet his two youngest held a treasured place in his heart. He stayed true to the final promise he had made to his beloved wife.

When Special One was seventeen, he was north of the valley with his ten older brothers watching the flocks. The night was clear and cold as the boys huddled around the campfire telling stories and trying to keep warm. It was late when the first wineskin was passed around the circle. The second and third were close behind. Special One kept an eye on the sheep as his brothers enjoyed the evening, but in time the brothers got loud and boisterous. Words were shouted, tempers flared; threats were hurled, punches connected. It would have been over and quickly forgotten, had not the ruckus spooked nearby sheep. They ran panic-stricken in every direction.

Special One herded them together and tried to calm them, but with wild bleating and blind fear they raced from their safe meadow toward a precipice. The teenager ran in front to turn them back. He waved his arms frantically. But the sheep were too frantic. They pushed madly forward, knocking down their protector. They did not even pause on the edge of the cliff. Each raced madly after the others until the entire flock lay lifeless on the sharp rocks at the foot of the drop.

Special One ran back to the camp in shock and horror.

Hundreds of sheep had plunged downward.

Broken and bloodied, they were piled, white wool glowing in the starlight.

A few feeble bleats could be heard.

"Help me!" he yelled at his brothers. "Maybe some can be saved. We have to try."

The ten older brothers lay about the fire, half-dressed in drunken disheveled sleep. Special One shook them and yelled at them and even threw cold water in their faces. The brothers mumbled incoherently and pushed him away. A few woke enough to stumble about before falling back to the ground. In frustration he returned to the base of the cliff in hopes of finding survivors, but those not dead were hopelessly mangled.

As the first light of day broke through, Special One walked with Promise-Keeper. "What shall I do?"

"Tell the truth."

"But if I tell my father, my brothers will hate me."

"There is nothing you can do to quench their jealousy. They will make your life difficult, but there will come a time when they will thank you for being their brother. Now, go to your father and say what must be told."

Special One rushed south to the Valley of Apples and stood alone before Wrestler.

"What has happened? Where are your brothers?" his horrified father asked.

Special One took a deep breath and told his father everything. Wrestler shook his head and covered his face. "Why can't my sons be trustworthy?"

"I'm sorry, Father."

"You did what you could. You will be rewarded and they will be reprimanded."

"No, Father, don't do that."

"Leave me. I don't want to hear anymore."

So Special One respectfully withdrew from his father's presence.

Each son felt the scorch of his father's wrath. But Special One received a long woolen coat dyed with the colors of the rainbow. Never had the brothers seen such a marvelous coat. No longer did they conceal their hatred for Special One.

The boy sat beside his father and ran his hands over the impressive coat. "It's like Promise-Keeper's banner across the sky," he said.

"I thought you would understand. Now you can remember the promise without waiting for rain and sun to mix," said Wrestler. "When you wear your coat think of Promise-Keeper's message: 'I am always close and I will always care.'"

Special One had dreamed clear and colorful and dramatic dreams for as long as he could remember. But soon after he received the rainbow coat his dreams took on a more vivid reality. He intuitively understood that these night visions were more than mere ordinary dreams.

The blue planet trembled as lightning flashed and thunder shook the night. A mighty wind howled from the north carrying with it a thick rolling dust which consumed the barren hills. Then Promise-Keeper clapped his cosmic hands and there was light. The wind made peace with the hills and the dust settled. Streaks of silver watered the dark soil and sprouts from freshly planted seeds burst through the moist earth. Tender shoots of wheat climbed toward the sun, growing golden before Special One's sleeping eyes. Suddenly twelve angels with twelve shining sickles appeared in the field. With wide and powerful strokes they harvested the wheat into twelve neat piles resting calmly on the stubbly ground. The twelve brothers stepped into the dream, each gathered a pile and tied it firmly together. A perplexed look crossed Special One's face as his bundle came to life and leapt from his hands and stood upright in the field, surveying all that lay before him. In quick succession the remaining eleven bundles came to life, leapt from the brothers' hands and encircled Special One's bundle. As the single sheaf stood tall and erect, the rest bowed before him.

"What a strange dream," said Special One.

"What foolishness," said his brothers.

"No, it's a gift from Promise-Keeper and full of meaning."

"What conceit. Do you really think that we will ever bow down before you?"

"I do not understand it, but I did not make it up," said Special One. "Promise-Keeper has revealed something about our future."

"You dreamer," the brothers said and shook their heads and walked away. The new name stuck to Special One as strongly as did the brothers' jealousy. That jealousy burned hotter after a new vision:

All was dark and he floated weightlessly through the boundlessness of space. Galaxies and constellations and comets spun through their divinely charted courses. The dreamer wore his multicolored coat and held hands with the universe. Then the sun and the moon and eleven stars blazed through the black. They sped toward him, sparks in the night growing larger and brighter. They seemed drawn toward him, as if they needed him. The planets surrounded the dreamer and the largest of the eleven said, "Save us." The sun winked at him with his father's eyes as the moon and stars orbited in reverence and submission.

"This dream is more absurd than the last," said the brothers. "If you think any of us will worship you, you are not clear-headed."

From that point Dreamer's ten older brothers looked for any opportunity to hurt or humiliate him. The opportunity came several full moons later when Wrestler sent Dreamer to check on his brothers. They were three days north tending the flocks on the land Wrestler had bought near the place of the portal.

Shining-One traveled openly with the brothers now. He had been close by ever since their drunken party around the campfire.

He struck at their heels.

He hissed in their ears.

He fueled their hatred.

When the ten saw Dreamer coming up the hill toward them, Shining-One recognized his opening to do something grand. Sliding out from a nearby rock he fanned the brothers' jealousy and outrage until it blazed bright on that lonely hillside. Then he slithered back to his wicked rock and gleefully watched evil consume the ten with marvelous, limitless hatred.

"Let's beat him," said a brother.

"And break his arms," said another.

"Let's torture him with poisonous scorpions," said one more as Shining-One smiled.

"Let's just kill him and be done with it."

"We'll throw the body down the old well," someone suggested.

Some cheered in agreement; others were not so sure.

"Father will suspect us."

"Not if we tell him a lion attacked his favorite. Then what will happen to Dreamer's dreams."

All had been seduced by the snake except the oldest brother. "I also hate Dreamer, but think what you're doing. Punishing him is one thing, murder is another. Throw him down the well. Beat him if you must, but I do not want his blood on my hands."

The brothers listened and thought and nodded. The tide had turned and Shining-One seethed. One by one they saw the eldest brother's point. Wickedness was still in their plan but not murder. The snake had not won the day as completely as he wished. The ten broke their circle and laid their trap.

They grabbed him and beat him and tore off his coat. They dropped Dreamer down the dry old well. Then the oldest went to the flocks while the rest sat down to eat and plan. Out of the heat shimmers appeared a caravan of desert people from the north, their camels laden with gold and grain.

"Where are you bound?" hailed one brother.

"South to the Land of Deltas."

"We have heard they need slaves there," called one.

"That's true. Do you have any for sale?"

"A young male, strong and smart."

"Let us see him."

The brothers took the desert people to the well. The travelers examined Dreamer. He stood erect, looking in disbelief at his brothers. They shunned his silent stare.

"Twenty pieces of silver."

"No, thirty."

"Twenty-five."

Hands bound, Dreamer walked off south toward the delta.

Hours later the oldest brother slipped to the well to save his brother and send him home. He disliked Dreamer, but he feared his brothers might yet decide to kill him. And the oldest was responsible for what the others did. He might forfeit his own life if harm befell Dreamer

"Where is Dreamer?" he demanded, rushing into camp.

"A sold slave among the desert people," answered the smugly pleased brothers.

"Father will disown us all."

"Not if we work our plan," said the brothers. They killed a goat and smeared the special coat in its blood. They took the rainbow cloth to their father. "See what we found. Have you seen Dreamer lately?"

"I sent him north to you," said Wrestler as he examined the bloodied coat.

"He must have been attacked by a lion."

The truth seemed impossible and obvious and awful. Heart-crushing sorrow blinded his eyes. "Dreamer. . .dead." The words fell and the coat slipped from numb fingers.

"This is a horrible tragedy, but you must go on."

"You go on with life," said their grieving father. "Lay me in my grave. Life is not worth living any longer."

Wrestler sluggishly turned from the brothers and went into his tent and wished to pass beyond this painful planet.

DOING RIGHT IS SELDOM REWARDED,
BUT A SINGLE COURAGEOUS STAND
GIVES THE WORLD HOPE.

CHAPTER 14

THE STAND

The desert people were kind—kinder to Dreamer than his brothers had been. They were also of Merchant's family, through a child of his old age. Dreamer made friends with these distant cousins. He joined them unbound before the night fire, telling stories and happenings of the blue planet. Dreamer shared the ancient tales of Garden-Maker while the desert people listened in awe of the one who lives beyond the sky and holds the stars in his hands.

Each evening they gathered as equals around the fire, but each morning Dreamer awoke as prisoner and property. For a cycle of the moon the desert people followed the ancient trade route to the great delta, following the steps Merchant had taken two hundred years before.

On the day the caravan passed the majestic granite gates of the City of the Sun, friendship and family gave way to business. Because of Dreamer's age and strength and intelligence, the desert people made a larger profit than they had expected. Slaves from the east were prized.

The wrinkled old men of the city watched the caravan pass through the marketplace. They loved to tell visitors, whether traders or slaves, about their country.

"For over a thousand years the first god-kings ruled the Land of Deltas," croaked the gravelly voice of the animated old man. "They ruled from an ancient city to the north and thought themselves immortal. They began this city as a place for priests who worship the land and the water and the sky."

"Do you know the one who is beyond the sky? The one called Garden-Maker and Promise-Keeper?"

The old man looked at Dreamer strangely. "I know no such names."

"What has become of all the god-kings?" he asked.

"All the immortal ones lie buried beneath amazing monuments across the great river." The old man pointed west.

"My ancestor Merchant came to this city and knew the god-kings," said Dreamer.

"The end of the first kings was sad. They faded in power, and the land fell to rebellion and anarchy. Invaders came across the Great Desert from the Mountains of the Dawn. But priest-kings from this city united the people and drove out the invaders. Now life is good and peaceful. Our leaders trade with all the world and encourage outsiders to live among us. They especially seek slaves from near the Mountains of the Dawn." The old man looked at Dreamer. "Outsiders like you are in short supply. Work hard and you will do very well."

Dreamer was quickly purchased by the captain of the Delta King's personal guards. The captain was born in the wetlands of the delta and trained in the skills of war from youth. He had risen to the highest post among the Delta King's soldiers. Under his command, elite swordsmen and spearmen secured the elaborate palace and protected the lives of the important. This was no easy task. Life in the City of the Sun might be good as the old man said, but there were always the dissatisfied who believed that anarchy and assassination would open the door to a better way. But the captain thrived on challenge. His soldiers watched closely the palace walls and shadowed even the least of the royal family. Anyone who wished to see the Delta King was personally questioned and searched by the captain. As long as he was in charge, all was safe.

For his dedication and enormous responsibility the captain was well-paid. His extravagant home adjoined the palace grounds so he could watch over everything under his protection. But he left many things within his own household unattended. He needed good servants to keep his domestic affairs in order and recognized in Dreamer his own gifts.

Dreamer started in the stable caring for his master's horses but his energy and leadership soon brought him into the captain's house. He scoured dishes and served meals. The captain's wife first noticed Dreamer's well-built frame and rugged strength as he waited on her family with confidence unseen in other servants. His dark eyes swept the room anticipating every need.

He was respectful and courteous without cowering.

He was direct and in control without threatening.

He was charming and eager to please without fawning.

And the captain's wife thought him so obsessively attractive that she eagerly awaited every meal. The captain saw him as trustworthy and competent. They agreed he had great potential—but for different reasons.

Dreamer increased in responsibility and status until he was head servant and the captain's personal attendant. Every aspect of running a smooth household was in his care. He answered only to the captain himself. Rarely in the City of the Sun had a servant enjoyed such power, but under Dreamer's able hand his master's estate flourished far beyond reason and expectation. Dreamer took no credit for his success. He explained to all who asked: "Every morning I awake before the dawn and walk with Promise-Keeper."

Her first flirtations were subtle, so subtle Dreamer did not notice. But it was harder to miss the special requests and flattery, the alluring smiles and prolonged glances. The captain's wife was lonely and lovely—beautiful of hair and refined of feature and voluptuous of figure. She seldom had the attention of her busy husband, but she could turn the eye of any man at will with her pouty lips and seductive manner. She knew she was irresistible and amused herself in the game of conquest. With perfectly applied cheek colorings and perfumed ointments and fine clothes she could have anything she wanted. Tonight she wanted Dreamer.

In the half-light of the lamps he could see that she had removed her tunic and wore only a sheer shawl of rare silk and a bright flaxen skirt tied loosely about her hips. All the household was to bed and the master journeyed with the Delta King to the ebony lands to the south. She smelled of perfume and wine.

"I have secured the house for the night, mistress," said Dreamer.

"I will feel safe if you accompany me to my chamber," she said softly and gently.

Leaning on Dreamer's shoulder and clinging to his arm, she whispered suggestive fantasies in the dark gallery that led to the sleeping rooms.

Dreamer closed his ears to her bewitching words as he focused his eyes on the floor and led the captain's wife forward as quickly as possible. He numbed his body to the gentle stroke of her fingers as they traced their way from his arm to his shoulder to his bare chest.

"Good night, my lady," said Dreamer at her chamber doorway. Before she could respond, he was gone.

She stared into the darkness after him and swore. Soon she would have Dreamer. His innocence was a fascinating challenge.

The wife continued to look for opportunities to charm and entice and seduce the virtuous. And to her frustration the head servant avoided her approaches and ignored her subtleties. But one evening when no one was around she wrapped her body in clinging silk, such as only royal women could afford. She washed and perfumed and then slipped from the evening shadows to touch his muscular shoulders as he bent, stylus in hand, over a wax tablet.

"Accompany me to my bed," she whispered.

"The way is safe, and you do not need my presence."

"Not to my chamber. . .to my bed." Her body trembled as she embraced him from behind.

The move startled Dreamer, so that he jumped and backed against the wall. His eyes darted back and forth seeking paths of escape.

"You are my mistress, and I obey your orders. But this I cannot do."

Her voice was more insistent and less gentle: "Please lay with me. I will make you glad." Her body blocked his way as she moved uncomfortably close to kiss his arm.

Dreamer ducked away. "You are married—and to my master. I know you are neglected but he trusts me and I will not betray him."

"So the problem is honor?" She twirled around and faced him with a derisive smile.

"The problem is who I am. I walk with Promise-Keeper, who first wove lives into one flesh. I cannot be unfaithful to him."

"You are my slave and do my bidding," she warned, . . .then more pleading in tone, "I know you want me and I need you."

"Wives must be faithful."

"Husbands should love their wives," she snapped back.

"Promise-Keeper sees all and I have pledged to remain pure. . . ."

"So you've never been with a woman?" she interjected, tightening her arms around his waist and pressing her soft curves firmly against him. "No wonder you are nervous."

". . .and. . .I will keep my pledge," Dreamer continued while gently nudging her away.

"I'm sure you will," said the captain's wife. "But we will see."

Dreamer turned away and fled to his quarters where he called to Promise-Keeper: "Please help me."

From that night, the captain's wife was ever more attentive and persistent, but Dreamer had now faced his desires and set his resolve.

The final attack came at the end of Dreamer's twenty-fourth year. While Dreamer bought at the market the mistress ordered each servant away from the house on some task. She left touches of expensive perfume where Dreamer worked and dressed to leave no doubt of her intent. She waited in hungry anticipation. As soon as he entered the room she clasped her arms around his neck and caressed his chest with her cheek.

"Please don't," he said.

"Relax," she cooed as she rubbed the tight muscles of his upper back. Emotions battled within him.

She was both beautiful and desirable.

She would not stop until he gave in to her.

She could cause great trouble if he refused.

He nearly melted beneath the weight of his temptation and her tender touch. But then he caught himself. What was he doing there? He spun around, confronted her face-to-face and spoke firmly, "No!"

"We will see," she said as she undid his linen shirt. "I know what you want."

"I want to please Promise-Keeper. That's what I want."

The woman grabbed at the belt that held his clothes together. His shirt opened and fell away, leaving his chest bare. He reached for his covering, but it was wrapped around her arm and he could not get it from her. To attack master or mistress meant death.

So he ran.

He didn't hesitate or look back.

He didn't even slow down.

"Come back!" she yelled. "You can't leave me. If you take another step you will regret it." She watched him flee with fury and frustration. Rejected, and by a slave? No! It was not to be tolerated!

She ripped her clothing, smeared the coloring powders on her face and screamed until servants ran from their work outside. They found her hysterically crying and screaming and wailing: "Dreamer attacked me. . .he tore my clothes. Look, he even left his clothing when I screamed for help."

Dreamer was under guard before the captain was summoned. The master was enraged by his wife's sobbing story. He had trusted Dreamer with everything. This young man was more than his head servant; he was a cherished friend. Now he would face a brutal death as he deserved. A slave attempting to rape his mistress? Yes, he would die slowly.

"How could he have betrayed me?" He slammed his fist to the table.

How, indeed? That Dreamer would do such a thing seemed inconceivable. He could assume that his wife was not a total innocent. He knew the servant gossip. He saw her flirtatious manner with men. He caught her glances toward Dreamer. But Dreamer was a man of honor and respect and integrity. No, this story did not fit the man. Now a dilemma: He could not accept the word of his servant over that of his wife. They would both be disgraced.

Dreamer escaped death, but he was locked away in the Delta King's prison. There was little chance of release—for at least as long as the captain lived.

CHAPTER 15

THE SILOS

The imperial prison was a solid and windowless stronghold—dark and dreary but not oppressive. Most prisoners were unfortunates in disfavor with the Delta King or his nobles. Man-killers and highwaymen seldom lived long enouth to stand inside the walls. Lesser thieves were simply whipped and sold. But these men awaited the king's pleasure and disposition—days or seasons of quiet boredom before sudden release or enslavement or death. In this temporary house they awaited their fate.

Few stayed so long as Dreamer. Four long summers Dreamer lay a forgotten prisoner and not once did he complain. He worked hard and did whatever the jailers asked. He was polite and respectful and caused no trouble. It was noticed that his presence calmed the fearful and quieted the terror-stricken. The captain's servant showed intelligence and sensitivity. Others came and went but Dreamer remained. Each morning he awoke before the dawn and walked among the sleepers in the sunless common room with Promise-Keeper. Each afternoon he told the ancient stories—

of Man and Woman,

of the choice and the exile,

of Walker and Builder and Land-Baron.

The more the jailers watched Dreamer, the more they trusted him. At first he was put in charge of a few cooperative inmates assigned to forced labor and then he supervised all of the workers. Finally he oversaw the feeding and care of everyone. That is how he came to meet the Delta King's personal butler and baker.

The butler and the baker had been responsible for a major banquet in the Hall of the Sun greeting foreign dignitaries from beyond the Mountains of the Dawn. But things had gone badly. The Delta King wanted to impress the ambassadors, so he had ordered the finest foods and the sweet-est wine. But spoiled meat had gotten into the baker's main course, and the wine had definitely soured. Both men were too busy to sample before serving, and ambassadors became offended and very ill. The two bowed low before their monarch and pleaded for mercy. The king demanded a reason for his disgrace. They mumbled and muttered and minimized their blame, which made the Delta King even more angry. He rose in rage, turned his back on the two and called the guards.

"Take them away and lock them up. I've had enough of their incompetence and disrespect. Get them out of here before I personally end their lives."

Thus the butler and baker were placed in the care of Dreamer. One day the two new prisoners were unusually withdrawn. Their faces were long and they ate little.

"Why are you so downhearted?" asked Dreamer.

"We've both had dreams," said the butler.

"Promise-Keeper is the giver of dreams. He solves the most elusive enigma."

"So where do we find Promise-Keeper?"

"He lives beyond the sky, but hears every word you utter. Tell me your dreams and he will show me their meanings." The butler began:

"I sat alone in the middle of the day when a vine sprouted from the ground right in front of me. It grew rapidly and split into three branches. Each branch budded and blossomed and burst into the plumpest clusters of grapes. I picked a cluster and squeezed the grapes into the king's golden goblet until the juice overflowed. The liquid sparkled in the midday sun and as I stirred the nectar it fermented into the sweetest wine the Land of Deltas had ever tasted. I handed the cup to the Delta King and he smiled."

"Let me tell you my dream," said the baker.

"I was walking toward the Delta King's palace with three wicker baskets full of fresh baked rolls. These baskets were balanced on my head and I was stepping very carefully to make sure none fell. But ravens circled directly above me and swept down on my baskets to steal my bread and threw everything out of balance."

"So what do our dreams mean?" asked the butler.

"In three days the Delta King will reinstate you to your former position and things will be just as they were before you came here," said Dreamer to the butler. The servant jumped up in delight and hugged Dreamer. "What can I do to repay you?"

"Thank Promise-Keeper. And tell the Delta King that I am innocent and am here only because I took a stand for what is right. Perhaps he will have mercy on me."

"I won't forget you," said the butler. "What of my friend the baker?"

Turning toward the baker he bowed his head and said quietly, "In three days the Delta King will execute you. He'll hang you from the hanging tree and the ravens will swoop down to pick your bones clean."

Three days later was the Delta King's birthday and the whole city celebrated. A huge feast filled the Hall of the Sun with every servant and employee of the palace joining in the merriment. At the peak of the party, the Delta King called for his butler and baker to be brought before him. The butler was reinstated and the baker was executed—just as Promise-Keeper said.

For two more summers Dreamer continued his quiet work among the inmates at the imperial prison. The butler always served the Delta King the sweetest wine and he never forgot to thank his master for reinstating him, but he did forget the teller of dreams. But Promise-Keeper did not forget.

One still night when the moon was full the Delta King's sleep was filled with vivid images:

He stood on the bank of the wide river of the great delta, watching his herds hiding themselves from the heat and humidity. Then seven contented and well-fed cows came out of the water to graze on the abundant marsh grass. A moment later seven more cows came out of the water, grotesque and emaciated—their ribs were prominent beneath paper-thin skin so that they looked more dead than alive. The seven grotesque cows limped to the seven contented cows, circled them like a lion moving in for its kill. Hungry eyes glared at well-fed bellies and shriveled mouths chewed imaginary cuds. One of the thin cows leaned forward and took a vicious bite from the plump side of a prosperous cow. Another thin cow took a bite and then another and another and another until the seven grotesque cows had devoured all the flesh of the well-fed cows.

The Delta King sat up with a start, his bed clothing damp with sweat and his heart pounding hard. "What a strange dream," he thought. Then he fell back to sleep and watched one more dream.

A stalk of corn grew up in the marshlands of the great delta. Seven ears of corn sprouted from that single stalk. They were fat and golden with a sweet smell that made the Delta King smile. Then seven more ears of corn grew on that same sturdy stalk, but these were stunted and shriveled and sickly. Yet these new ears would not die quietly. Somehow they reached out and swallowed the seven healthy ears.

The Delta King left his bed and paced his chamber through the night. These were no ordinary dreams. He must learn their message. Shortly after the sun peaked into his domain, he summoned the stargazers to the palace.

"What do these dreams mean?" he demanded. "What are they trying to tell me?"

The royal stargazers listened intently and calculated the alignment of the planets with the constellations and studied their charts. But the dreams remained a mystery. "We don't know their meaning," said the stargazers to the Delta King. "This is from beyond the sky."

The Delta King's butler heard the answer. "I know a man who walks with the one who lives beyond the sky and who holds the stars in his hands," he said.

"Who is this man? And where can I find him?"

"He is Dreamer and you hold him in the imperial prison though he is one of the best men I have known. When I was in the prison Dreamer told me the meaning of my dream and it came about exactly as he said."

The Delta King immediately called the captain of his bodyguards and commanded, "Bring Dreamer before me."

"But he is held for attacking my wife."

"My butler says he is innocent."

"I have declared him a criminal."

"I wonder. Why did you not have this 'criminal' executed for such a crime? Bring him to me quickly or you will take his place."

Scrubbed clean with new clothes and a freshly shaved face, Dreamer bowed before the Delta King.

"Last night I had two dreams," the Delta King said, "and the stargazers fail to tell me their meaning. But my butler says you walk with the one who lives beyond the sky and who knows all things."

"What your butler said is true. Tell me your dreams and Promise-Keeper will show me their meaning."

The Delta King told him every detail of the two dreams and when he finished all eyes in the room were fixed on Dreamer. But Dreamer was unconcerned. His eyes gazed beyond the sky and his ears heard the whispers of the infinite. To everyone else in the room the silence was uncomfortably heavy and grew heavier.

Suddenly Dreamer's eyes returned to the room and he spoke to the king. "Your two dreams are different pictures of the same future. The fat cows and the fat corn represent seven fat years with healthy cattle and abundant crops. But the good times will be followed by seven years of famine. The thin cows and the shriveled corn will swallow up all that came before. The famine will ravage every family and scar the land."

"So what does Promise-Keeper say we should do?" asked the king.

"Search the land for a wise and discerning heart and appoint that person over every harvest. Build large silos throughout the countryside and for the next seven years gather a portion of all the land produces. Store this reserve in the silos and when famine curses the soil, sell food to all in need."

The Delta King turned to his advisors and asked, "Where can we find a wise one we can trust with such a commission?"

The advisors looked at each other but said nothing. The Delta King shook his head at his advisors' lack of advice.

"Oh great king," said the captain of the guard. "I would ask a private audience to give you what may be helpful news."

The king studied the captain and then ordered the council room cleared. He listened to the story of the captain for some time, then summoned his council and Dreamer into his presence.

He turned to Dreamer. "Since Promise-Keeper has shown you the meaning of my dreams and the insight to know what to do, so I place you in charge of the harvests. I also grant you the position of prime minister over the mighty Land of Deltas. You shall be in charge of the welfare of my land, and all must obey your orders. Only I shall be your superior."

All the people in the room shouted honors to the Delta King and the new prime minister, though they wondered why a convicted criminal was so elevated. As the shouts rang out the captain quietly left the room, fearful of revenge and anticipating humiliation. Dreamer saw him leave and as soon as he was alone sent two guards for the captain. The guards didn't question the prime minister's order but brought back their commanding officer. With a guard on each side the captain returned without resistance. He held his head high and looked directly into Dreamer's eyes.

"I have been your slave and for six summers your prisoner, and now I am your superior," began Dreamer. "Therefore listen to the full truth that I was a trustworthy servant. I never touched nor threatened your wife. I was completely innocent in this matter. I was your friend and you treated me as a traitor. I think you know these things and may have told some of them to the king. For that and for sparing my life I should be grateful, but why did you treat me so?"

The captain lowered his head. "My life is in your hands." The captain bowed low before the prime minister and kissed his sandaled feet.

"Your life is in Promise-Keeper's hands, not mine," Dreamer said.

The formal ceremony elevating Dreamer to his high position took place on the expansive front steps of the palace in the midmorning sunshine. People crowded the streets, cheering and throwing flowers, as almost every inhabitant of the City of the Sun joined the celebration. When the Delta King stood and raised his arms the people hushed. The king removed his signet ring, the symbol of royal authority, and slipped it onto Dreamer's finger. Attendants draped the prime minister in the finest linen and the king set a heavy gold chain around his neck. All the people bowed before him as the king declared Dreamer to be second-in-command of everything within the boundaries of the Land of Deltas.

So at the age of thirty Dreamer went from prisoner to prime minister. Soon he married the daughter of the chief stargazer. Dreamer told his wife of Promise-Keeper and in time she learned to trust the one who held the stars in his hands rather than the stars themselves. She loved her husband and gave him two healthy sons. During the seven good years the new prime minister worked at an exhausting pace and traveled throughout the land building large silos in each town and supervising the collection of a portion of every harvest. By the end of the fat years Dreamer had stored away so much food that the people could not imagine needing such a surplus.

But the following year the east winds scorched the crops and the wide river that fed the delta shrunk to a fraction of its size. The soil dried out and cracked and blew away. The plants shriveled and the cattle died and the people grew hungry. The famine spread throughout the entire country and far beyond.

Then the people looked to the silos overflowing with grain. Dreamer opened the doors to the storehouses and sold their contents. Many who would have starved were thus saved and word spread throughout the blue planet of the wise man in the Land of Deltas who had gathered grain for all in need. So even in the worst of famines there was hope.

And this hope reached as far as the Valley of Apples.

HOWEVER DARK A SITUATION,
PATIENCE AND PROVIDENCE
CAN BRIGHTEN THAT DARKNESS
INTO A POINT OF HOPE.

CHAPTER 16

THE REUNION

Wrestler watched the Valley of Apples die. For many months there had been no rain, not a drop. The greens turned brown and the soft became brittle and a cruel sun sucked life from the most fertile meadows of the high ridge. This was the greatest famine ever on the blue planet, greater than even Merchant had faced centuries before. Wrestler rubbed his dried-out eyes with a wrinkled hand and released a long sigh, low and tired. He scooped up a fistful of dry dirt. It fell through his trembling fingers as he shook his head and wished there was enough water in his body to cry. His paradise was fading—

his two wives were dead and his special son had been torn apart by a lion;

his brother's children attacked his herds;

his crops were worthless and his ten oldest sons seemed always in trouble.

The only good news was that the prime minister of the Land of Deltas was selling grain to whomever asked. He sent his ten oldest sons south.

"Why does your youngest son always stay at home?" asked one of the brothers.

"It is because my sons have never earned my trust. As men you act without wisdom. Even your words on the death of Special One do not satisfy me. Only one child is the joy of my eyes. I will not allow your jealousy or rashness to bring him to harm."

The ten loaded their camels and donkeys in guilty silence, tasting bitter regret in their mouths. It was a slow trip south through charring heat and waterless wilderness to the great delta. They were speechless with awe as they rode through the majestic granite gates of the beautiful City of the Sun. At the same moment Dreamer rested from the heat in his administrative chamber, which looked down on the busy streets. Idly watching the broad way to the market and grain silos, he noticed the dust-covered foreigners and their vaguely familiar walk and dress. Dreamer leaned out into the sun and watched closely. Twenty summers had passed. Time and elements had chiseled lines on their faces, but they were his brothers. He started for the stairs, excited to embrace his past. But then something hissed behind him and Dreamer stopped.

"Remember what they did to you?" whispered the snake. "They beat you and threw you down a well and sold you as a slave."

"How could they do that to their own brother?" said Dreamer.

"Hatred!" Shining-One hissed. "They hated you and they always will. But you can protect yourself and have revenge."

"But they are my brothers."

"Half-brothers," corrected the snake as he slithered away.

When the brothers reached the silos the prime minister himself stood with the grain sellers, robed in purple with a heavy gold chain around his neck. They bowed until their faces touched the ground and Dreamer remembered his long-ago dreams.

"Get up," the high official demanded. "Where are you from?"

"From far to the north," said the brothers. "A place called the Valley of Apples."

"Why have you stolen across our eastern border?"

"We are humble shepherds grown thin from famine. We have come to buy food. That is all."

"Do you take me for a fool?" yelled Dreamer. "You are spies who are here to learn our defenses."

"No, that's not true. We aren't spies—just ten brothers from the Valley of Apples."

"You are all liars."

"No," they insisted. "Our father and youngest brother wait at home for us to return with food."

"Prove it to me," said Dreamer.

"How?" asked the brothers.

"Let me consider. But in the meantime confine them." Guards surrounded the frightened brothers.

"Have mercy on us. All we wanted is food."

"You will get the same mercy you have given," said Dreamer. "Take them to the imperial prison."

The guards roughly escorted the prisoners away. Dreamer returned to his work, collapsed in an ornately carved chair and buried his face in his hands. "How can I treat my brothers like this?"

In the far corner of the room the snake snickered.

Three days later the prisoners faced the accusing prime minister.

"I have considered your claims," said Dreamer. "And I have a proposal. Accept it and you can prove you are not spies. Reject it and you will be executed as the sun begins its daily journey.

"I will select one of you to remain as my prisoner. The rest of you can leave with enough grain to feed your households. Return with your youngest brother and I will release your imprisoned brother. Fail to return and your brother dies."

The ten had no choice but to agree and Dreamer chose the second-born to remain. Guards bound him in shackles around his arms and feet, and led him away. The rest were released. Their bags were filled with grain and loaded on donkeys they had brought to carry back their purchases. The nine sadly thanked the prime minister for his mercy and generosity. They promised to return to prove they'd told the truth.

Dreamer stood at his window and watched his brothers' caravan pass through the granite gates. Tears welled in his eyes as he thought about the Valley of Apples where his father and youngest brother awaited grain from the delta. Dreamer looked beyond the sky and sighed, "Promise-Keeper, please bring my brothers back."

That evening, just before the sun splashed into the western sea, the nine brothers set up camp. As they unloaded the grain from the donkeys they discovered silver coins at the top of each bag. They all gathered around the grain and counted out the coins. They had received back the money they had paid the prime minister for the grain.

"We are in great trouble now," said the oldest.

"There must be something we can do," said another.

"We didn't put the money into our bags. But how can we prove it?" said another.

"The prime minister already thinks we're spies. Now he will think we are thieves and traitors," said the oldest.

"Let us return home fast and hope they never discover their error."

The nine brothers faced their father and told him the whole story of the prime minister's accusations and their imprisonment and the silver coins in the their grain bags. Wrestler listened in silence, his face tense and his lips tightly pressed together. When his boys finished, he bowed his head and mumbled, "I can't do it. I just can't do it. I lost Dreamer and now I have lost my second-born. I cannot risk my youngest."

"Your second-born isn't lost, he is locked in the imperial prison in the City of the Sun. All we have to do is return with the youngest and the prime minister will release him."

"But what if he doesn't? What if they have already killed him and now wait to harm the youngest?"

"Let me go with the youngest to get the second-oldest released," said the oldest son.

"I just can't do it. That is my decision." Wrestler stood up, turned his back on the brothers and disappeared into his tent.

A year passed and all the grain was gone. Wrestler called the nine older brothers together. "Sons, the famine shows no sign of breaking. I must send you back to the Land of Deltas for more grain."

"The prime minister will not sell us grain unless we bring back the youngest," said one of the brothers.

The fourth born stood up. He was the strongest and most courageous of the brothers. "Father if we do not go, you and the youngest and all our families will die of starvation. If the nine of us go without the youngest, the prime minister will kill us as spies. Send the youngest in my care and I will guarantee his safe return. I'll lay down my life to bring him back."

Wrestler relented. "Be wary and watchful. Carry expensive gifts and pack double the silver you need so you can pay back what was found in your bags. And keep your youngest brother with you always." Then Wrestler placed his right hand on the fourth-born's shoulder. "May Promise-Keeper walk with you and protect you and bring you all back quickly."

The nine sons and the youngest rode their camels south. Not long after they passed through the majestic granite gates of the city they were surrounded by armed guards and escorted to the prime minister's home.

"What have we done wrong?" asked the oldest.

"You seem to have done as you were asked," said the prime minister's head servant. "The city guards were told to watch for you and bring you here whenever you arrived."

"But when we left before we found silver coins in the top of our bags of grain. We did not mean to take them."

"The prime minister ordered your silver returned to you. He did not want your money."

"So why were we brought here?" asked the oldest.

"You are to wash the travel dust off your bodies and dress in clean clothes and go to the banqueting room," said the head servant. As the brothers washed, a familiar face appeared in the doorway. The oldest brother saw Second-Born first and with a shout of glee the two embraced. Soon all the brothers crowded around with many questions:

Had Second-Born been well treated?

When had he been released?

Why were they all the prime minister's guests?

When the sun reached its highest point in the sky, they were joined by the prime minister. He greeted each, asking them about their trip and assuring them that they were not suspected spies. The brothers gave their gifts and Dreamer led them into the main banquet room. A long table covered with fine linen was laid with such meats and breads and wine as they had not seen for many years. Each brother was led to a designated spot by servants who knew their names. The brothers stared at each other in amazement.

"How do they know our names?" asked one.

"How did they know to seat us by order of our ages?" wondered another.

"Let us not worry over questions we cannot answer," said the oldest. "We have the meal of our lives to enjoy."

The eleven brothers and Dreamer feasted together. They ate and drank and visited until darkness fell and sleep hung heavy in their eyes. The next morning the eleven brothers awoke to find their bags plump with grain and strapped on their donkeys. They thanked their mysterious host and said their good-byes and headed home.

Later the prime minister called in his head servant. "Take fifty armed guards and go after the family that ate here. Search their bags for my silver cup."

The head servant chased the brothers north, circled their party and confronted them with the accusation.

"We have taken nothing," said the oldest. "Look through all our belongings. If you find anything we have taken, may that person be executed and the rest of us be your slaves."

"No," said the prime minister's servant. "But if we find my master's silver cup in one of your belongings, then that person will return to the City of the Sun with me and will become my master's lifelong slave. The rest of you will be free to go your way."

Each bag was unloaded and each string untied starting with the oldest and ending with the youngest. When the servant came to the last bag he pulled out the prime minister's silver cup. All stared at the youngest in disbelief.

"What have you done?" demanded the oldest.

"Nothing," said the youngest. "I did not take it."

The armed guards surrounded him and bound him in shackles. The rest argued but could do nothing except follow the guards back the way they had come.

"Why have you betrayed me?" accused the prime minister. "I was generous and look how you have treated me."

"We do not know how your silver cup got in the youngest's bag," said the oldest. "However, it was there and so we have all returned to be your slaves."

"Only the one who stole the cup must pay the price. The rest of you are free to return to your father."

"Please, exalted prime minister," said the fourth-born with utmost respect. "The youngest brother is my father's closest son. It will kill him if we don't return with his last-born. I beg you to let the youngest go and take me instead, and I will serve you faithfully."

"Stop," interrupted the prime minister, tears welling in his eyes. Then he turned to the guards. "Release the youngest and leave the room so that I can speak alone with the brothers."

Tears now streamed down his face and his body shook with emotion. All the guards and servants quickly left the room in wonder. The brothers looked on in silence until the fourth-born stepped forward and said, "Please, believe us that we did not take the silver cup."

"I do," said the prime minister. "I put my cup in your bag as I placed the coins there."

"Why?" asked the fourth-born.

"Because I am your brother, Dreamer, the one you sold to the caravan."

The eleven looked into the face of their long-lost brother and recognized him at last. They pulled back in fear and humiliation.

"I have not brought you back to harm you," said the prime minister. "Long ago I forgave you. Promise-Keeper has taken the wrong that you did and turned it into great good. He sent me to the Land of Deltas so many people, including you, would not starve."

Slowly the meaning of his words was realized.

Finally the past could be discussed.

At last the hurts and jealousies of youth could be exchanged for love.

"Hurry to tell Father what you have seen. Another five years of famine remain. I will provide everything you need."

The Delta King heard that the prime minister's brothers were in the City of the Sun and he called for Dreamer. "I will give them the best grazing land in the eastern delta," he said. "Send carts and donkeys north to bring back your entire family, especially your father. Tell him that the Delta King personally requests that he and his sons and their families come to the eastern delta."

The brothers immediately accepted the Delta King's invitation and traveled home for their father. But Wrestler did not believe his sons.

"Dreamer is alive and living well in the Land of Deltas," said the first-born.

"I held his bloodstained coat twenty summers ago. If he was somehow alive, he would have come home years ago."

"He was a slave and then in prison. But now he leads the Land of Deltas as prime minister, second to no one but the Delta King himself."

"First Dreamer is a slave, then a prisoner and now prime minister? What sort of story is this?"

"A true one," said the first-born. "See that caravan coming behind us. It is sent from the Delta King to bring us to his land."

"It all happened just like Dreamer dreamed years ago," said the fourth-born earnestly. "We all bowed down before him. And we didn't even know what we were doing."

"My son alive," repeated Wrestler in ecstasy. "Before I die I must look on the face of Special One."

With his belongings packed in the sturdy carts sent by the Delta King and his livestock driven ahead, Wrestler took his final look at the Valley of Apples. It had been a paradise. Why had Promise-Keeper let such beauty wither? He looked behind to see some of his eleven sons and their eleven wives and almost fifty of their children. Already some of his grandchildren had children. Back at the place of the portal Promise-Keeper had told him his descendants would be as plentiful as the stars. He certainly had made a beginning.

Two days later, Wrestler stopped the caravan and slowly climbed from his camel. His family watched in silence as he took out his knife and sacrificed a spotless newborn lamb to Promise-Keeper on the stone altar of his father. Promise-Keeper looked down from beyond the sky and smiled. A wind blew in from the Great Sea and whirled around the old man. "Wrestler. Wrestler," called the voice on the wind.

"I am here," replied the old man.

"I am Promise-Keeper and I will protect you and your children and your children's children. Walk with me and I will lead you to your lost son in the Land of Deltas."

So Wrestler followed Promise-Keeper to the fertile delta. Over parched land it was a difficult journey for the livestock and almost as hard for the old man. Wrestler neither gave up nor slowed down. His muscles ached and his back hurt and his body slumped from exhaustion in the dry and sun-scorched wilderness. "I will see my son," he mumbled to himself. "I will see Special One, stolen from my side so long ago."

"Follow me," whispered Promise-Keeper.

As the caravan entered the flat fertile lands of the eastern delta the brothers noticed a dust cloud in the southwest. A group of riders was coming with speed along the trade road.

The gathered family watched the upheaval of dust with concern as it moved closer.

"Do you think we're in trouble?" asked one of the son's wives.

"No," said the oldest. "We are doing as Dreamer and the Delta King told us to do. We were given this land to raise flocks."

In the billowy brown dust were a few of the Delta King's horsemen. In the lead was a powerful white horse, such as the brothers had seen occasionally in the Delta King's service.

Then the youngest leaned forward, his attention focused on the olive-skinned horseman. "It is Dreamer," he shouted.

Not until the horses were about to collide with the camels and carts did the prime minister pull back on the reins. Dreamer jumped to the ground, and he and his father collapsed into each other's embrace. Time stilled for the father and son who had lost twenty years. Guilt-ridden faces were among those who looked on. Ten brothers asked, "How could we have sold our brother?"

But a splintered family was at last reunited.

"All that I have asked of Promise-Keeper has come to pass, even what I thought was impossible," said Wrestler. "I am ready to walk with him beyond the sky."

"Not yet," said Dreamer. "After so long without a father, let us all live awhile in this new land and laugh and love and labor as one. There is much I want to share before you walk beyond this planet."

Father and son stared into each other's tearstained eyes and saw the future of a great nation—a nation guided by the one who is infinite and eternal and all-powerful.

CHAPTER 17

THE BLESSING

The Delta King studied the olive wrinkles of the prime minister's father with a look of grave respect. The king sat tall and regal on his jeweled throne. The white-haired Wrestler silently leaned on his oak staff in the semidarkness of the long and narrow room. He spoke to the king while regarding with curiosity the two bronze spearmen who stood statuelike at his side.

"You must be the eldest of a long-lived people," said the Delta King. The small lamps about the throne reflected off the golden walls and laid the visitor's long, thin shadow across the floor.

"My father and his father were older when they left this planet," answered Wrestler.

"Come, tell me how you live such a long and rich life," said the Delta King as he motioned Wrestler forward.

"My days have been difficult, but I wake every morning before the sun and walk with Promise-Keeper. He gives me strength and each heartbeat belongs to him."

"How does one meet this Promise-Keeper?"

"He lives beyond the sky and holds the stars in his hands. But he knows you already," Wrestler added. "He knows about all things."

The Delta King dismissed his guards and all in the hall. He left his throne and guided Wrestler toward the courtyard garden. There they spoke in low tones.

"I have always wondered what secrets hide beyond the sky," the Delta King admitted when they were alone.

"More than we imagine," agreed Wrestler.

Two monarchs talked as brothers until the sun cast a red glow on the paving stones. Wrestler placed his hand on the shoulder of the great king. "I will ask Promise-Keeper to grant you long life. And if you come to walk with him he will one day show you the secrets beyond the sky." They parted in mutual honor that endured until their final breaths.

The great famine ended at the end of the seven years. For twelve summers more Wrestler watched his sons shepherd their flocks in the fertile flatlands of the eastern delta. Life was gracious and as the years passed new generations began running across the fields—

laughing,

playing,

growing strong.

Often Dreamer traveled north from the City of the Sun to visit his father and the two spoke of many things, but what they enjoyed the most was talking about their early morning walks with Promise-Keeper.

One afternoon shortly before Dreamer was to return to the City of the Sun, his father pulled him close.

"Soon I will leave this planet, and I ask your promise of one thing before I go."

"If it is within my power I will do whatever you ask."

"Carry my body north to the Valley of Apples. Set me beside my father and grandfather."

"I will," said Dreamer as he embraced his father.

Several months later Wrestler became sick. His breath was shallow and his body weak. Dreamer rushed to his father's bedside with his own two sons, who were themselves now men. Wrestler opened his eyes and motioned his favorite forward. "Promise-Keeper appeared to me at the place of the portal and blessed me. He said my children would be as plentiful as the stars. He also gave to me the new land west of the Winding River and the Salty Sea. Don't forget the land."

"I won't."

"Now let me see the faces of your sons. They're both so young and handsome." Wrestler placed a hand on the head of each boy. "May Promise-Keeper, who walked with my father and his father, walk with these two. As they shepherd their flocks, may he shepherd them. And as his angels have protected me, may his angels guard their footsteps."

All of the brothers gathered around his bed. He cleared his throat.

"This is my last day on this planet and these are my last words. When

I'm finished Dreamer knows what to do with me. But before I go let me remind you that this is not our land—we are only visitors here, guests of the Delta King. There will come a time when we must turn our eyes north and return to the land Promise-Keeper has given to us. We are a small people now, but one day we will be as plentiful as the stars. It all begins with the twelve of you."

Then Wrestler blessed his twelve sons, starting with the oldest he faced each and placed his shaky hands on their shoulders and looked into their eyes. In slow thought-out words he spoke in a soft voice from his heart and set a challenge for their future. When he finished, he laid his tired head on his pillow and closed his eyes. His breathing grew ragged and faint as his spirit prepared to leave the weary body and walk beyond the sky with Promise-Keeper. His sons crowded around him, speaking words of love. Wrestler smiled and a peace softened the harshness the years had etched on his face. His sons thought he smiled at them, but the joy was for something they could not see. Wrestler looked into the face of Promise-Keeper and touched the hands that hold the stars.

Dreamer buried his face in his father's empty chest and wept. For seventy days the brothers and their children and their children's children mourned. The body was prepared in the manner of royalty of the Land of Deltas. Then a royal funeral procession passed before the Delta King and all the dignitaries of his court. Fifty horseman escorted the body of Wrestler through the massive granite gates of the capital City of the Sun. Weeks later the twelve brothers and their families let their last tears fall for their father as they made their way to the cave of the ancestors at the west end of the Valley of Apples. They laid Wrestler beside his wife, the older of the two sisters. Nearby lay the bones of his parents and their parents.

Half a century later Dreamer lay on his deathbed while his brothers and children gathered near.

"We were foolish and hard-hearted and evil when we sold you to the caravan," admitted the brothers.

"But see what Promise-Keeper did to turn that to good," said Dreamer.

"What will we do without you?" said his children. "The people of the delta respect you but we mean nothing to them."

"Follow Promise-Keeper however hard the days. New Delta Kings may treat you cruelly but a day will come when you will be a great nation.

When that time comes, watch for the man who comes with a new name for Promise-Keeper. He will lead you home. And when you go, take my remains with you. Lay me in the cave of my ancestors next to my father and grandfather and great-grandfather."

"We will do as you wish."

"Now is my time to walk beyond the sky with the one who holds the stars in his hands."

"Why is Promise-Keeper so important?" asked a young boy, a child of Dreamer's grandchildren.

Dreamer was growing weak. His breathing labored and his eyes dimmed but now he grew more alert and turned to face the little one. "It is because. . ." Dreamer started, slowly and carefully, ". . .because he was the beginning and he will be the end."

"The beginning of what?"

"Everything. Before he was Promise-Keeper he was Garden-Maker. He is infinite. . .and eternal. . .and. . .and. . ."

Dreamer's eyes were fixed on his father who waved him forward. With his sentence unfinished, he stepped from his body and beyond the blue planet.

The oldest brother closed the lids of Dreamer's eyes and finished the final phrase, ". . .And all-powerful."

The departed one's children and grandchildren sobbed and tears streamed down the brothers' faces.

Suddenly the sun sparkled through the windows and raindrops sprinkled over the eastern delta. Dreamer's family moved out of the great house of the prime minister and their sad faces felt the refreshing drops of moisture. Above them sun and showers intermingled in an amazing multicolored banner across the sky. The brothers remembered a coat they had seen long ago. The children thought of one of their father's favorite stories— Builder and his boat and the rainbow of promise.

"What does the rainbow mean?" those same children had asked many years before as they sat on their father's knees.

Dreamer always smiled and looked up beyond the sky. And with a look that knew more than he said, he recited the words that his father had learned from his father: "No matter how distant Promise-Keeper may seem, he is always close and he will always care."

EPILOGUE

It was late.

The embers of the dying fire glowed among the ashes as the darkness hung heavy over the camp. For thirty nights the old man with the long gray beard had circled the flames and recited the history. For thirty nights a small crowd sat cross-legged on the dry, sandy ground listening to the stories and meditating on their meaning. There was much to learn about the one who lives beyond the sky and holds the stars in his hands, the one who was first called Garden-Maker and then Promise-Keeper.

The old man stopped and breathed deeply. Then he wrapped a simple wool blanket around his shoulders and quietly disappeared into the shadows. They watched him go, this respected old man of a hundred wrinkles who shared the truth of the ancient scrolls. They had lost their homes, but as long as they had the writings and teachers to tell the stories they would have a history and a future.

The few lingered around the red-hot embers, staring at the glow and listening to a wolf call its mate.

Their month of stories was over, but there were more stories to tell, stories for other nights in other months. The few knew that the embers would soon cool and sleep would call them to their tents, but they waited silently, listening for a breeze that would brush their faces with the whisper, "I am here."

BEHIND THE STORIES . . .

Bible texts, most from the Book of Genesis, inspired the stories in this volume. The corresponding Bible passages are:

The Garden	Genesis 2:1–15
The Woman	Genesis 2:18–25
The Revolt	Ezekiel 28:11–19, Isaiah 14:12–14
The Choice	Genesis 3:1–7
The Exile	Genesis 3:8–24
The Boys	Genesis 4:1–8
The Outlaw	Genesis 4:9–24
The Walker	Genesis 5:21–24
The Builder	Genesis 6:5–12
The Boat	Genesis 6:13–22
The Rainbow	Genesis 7:17–9:17
The Gateway to Heaven	Genesis 10:8–10, 11:1–9
The Land-Baron	Book of Job
The Merchant	Genesis 11:27–12:3
The Caravan	Genesis 12:4–9
The Famine	Genesis 12:10–20
The Parting	Genesis 13
The Rescue	Genesis 14
The Promise	Genesis 15–17
The City	Genesis 18–19
The Son	Genesis 21–22
The Bride	Genesis 23–24
The Twins	Genesis 25–27
The Escape	Genesis 28:1–31:23
The Return	Genesis 31:24–33:20, 35:1–15
The Dreamer	Genesis 35:16–27, 37:1–36
The Stand	Genesis 39:1–23
The Silos	Genesis 40–41
The Reunion	Genesis 42–46
The Blessing	Genesis 47–50